HEART TO HEART ABOUT MEN

WORDS OF ENCOURAGEMENT FOR WOMEN OF INTEGRITY

NANCY GROOM

NAVPRESS

BRINGING TRUTH TO LIFE
NavPress Publishing Group
P.O. Box 35001, Colorado Springs, Colorado 80935

P9-CPX-904

The Navigators is an international Christian organization. Our mission is to reach, disciple, and equip people to know Christ and to make Him known through successive generations. We envision multitudes of diverse people in the United States and every other nation who have a passionate love for Christ, live a lifestyle of sharing Christ's love, and multiply spiritual laborers among those without Christ.

NavPress is the publishing ministry of The Navigators. NavPress publications help believers learn biblical truth and apply what they learn to their lives and ministries. Our mission is to stimulate spiritual formation among our readers.

© 1995 by Still Point Press, Inc.
All rights reserved. No part of this publication may be reproduced in any form without written permission from NavPress, P. O. Box 35001, Colorado Springs, CO 80935.
Library of Congress Catalog Card Number: 94-12883
ISBN 08910-98526

Some of the anecdotal illustrations in this book are true to life and are included with the permission of the persons involved. All other illustrations are composites of real situations, and any resemblance to people living or dead is coincidental.

Unless otherwise identified, all Scripture quotations in this publication are taken from the HOLY BIBLE: NEW INTERNATIONAL VERSION® (NIV®). Copyright © 1973, 1978, 1984 by International Bible Society. Used by permission of Zondervan Publishing House. All rights reserved.

Groom, Nancy.
    Heart to heart about men : words of encouragement for women of integrity / Nancy Groom.
    p.   cm.
    ISBN 0-89109-852-6
    1. Men—United States—Psychology. 2. Masculinity (Psychology)—United States. 3. Sex differences (Psychology). 4. Man-woman relationships—United States. 5. Christian women—United States—Interviews. I. Title.
HQ1090.G77 1994
306.7—dc20   94-12883
                                                      CIP
Printed in the United States of America

2 3 4 5 6 7 8 9 10 11 12 13 14 15 / 00 99 98 97 96

FOR A FREE CATALOG OF
NAVPRESS BOOKS & BIBLE STUDIES,
CALL 1-800-366-7788 (USA)
or 1-416-499-4615 (CANADA)

CONTENTS

To Bill, who loves me

Acknowledgments

Almost never is a book written single-handedly. But this book in particular could not have been produced without the sacrificial involvement of many people.

Vision and oversight for this project came from my publishing consultant, Steve Griffith, along with Steve Webb of NavPress, and Rick Kingham, Pete Richardson, and Mary Guenther of Promise Keepers. Their direction and encouragement charted my path; I am much indebted to them.

I also deeply appreciate the women who talked with me about their relationships with men. I am rich with the memories of our interviews and glad to tell some of their stories: Valerie Bell, Jane Berry, Dale Hanson Bourke, Rachael Crabb, Peg De Boer, Jody Engel, Mary Farrar, Barbara Feil, Barbara Fletcher, Jan Frank, Penny Freeman, Cynthia Heald, Cinny Hicks, Mary Kassian, Annemarie Landman, Pat Landman, Karen Lee-Thorp, Pat Palau, Leanne Payne, Kathy Peel, Holly Phillips, Pamela Reeve, Edith Schaeffer, Luci Shaw, Mary Swierenga, Judy Vander Plate, and Susan Yates.

The necessary details regarding travel, finances, and

interview transcription fell into place because of the competent efforts of Jennifer Mecho, Elizabeth Jansen, Terry and Sandi Henry, and Barbara Kling. I am grateful for their fine work and "extra mile" efforts.

My pastor, Al LaCour, offered thoughtful feedback on the early drafts of my manuscript, providing a much appreciated male perspective and wise theological insight. His kindness has been as supportive as his wisdom.

Liz Heaney, editor for this book, shaped and molded my manuscript with professionalism and kind sensitivity. She offered her friendship along with her competence, and I have been blessed by both. Nancy Burke, Deena Davis, Debby Weaver, and Kathy Yanni added their kindness and editorial skills to Liz's; I could not have managed without them.

I especially thank God for my good friends, Jody Engel, Penny Freeman, and Mary Ann Ulmer. They grappled alongside me with heart and mind to clarify the content of this book, praying all the while that my husband, my computer, and my sanity would survive its birthing. Every woman should have such friends.

There are no words adequate to convey my gratitude to my husband, Bill, for his invaluable suggestions and sacrificial support. He endured with gracious kindness not only my prolonged absences in the interviewing stage of this project but also my neglected household chores (which he shouldered) as I cloistered myself to write against deadlines. More than that, he delights in who I am, stands strong on my behalf, and models to me in countless ways the heart and voice of God. I could ask for no greater gifts.

Finally, I must acknowledge my indebtedness to the men and women in my church and around the country who have prayed for me and for this project from beginning to end. God knows their names and their reward. My heartfelt thanks to them and to Him whose splendid grace is the only reason I have anything at all worth saying.

INTRODUCTION
WHAT'S GOING ON HERE?

The sun was taking its own sweet time disappearing behind the Colorado Rockies, waving its colorful farewell to the day across the clouds of a slowly darkening sky. A serene Saturday dusk crept over the University of Colorado campus in Boulder, Colorado, but from my place in the press box above crowded Folsom Stadium, I could barely see the falling shadows for my gathering tears.

I had been invited to attend this Promise Keepers men's conference to get a glimpse of one way God is coming to His sons in these final days of the twentieth century. Promise Keepers, an organization founded in 1990 by former University of Colorado head football coach Bill McCartney, had convened several conferences like this one, inviting men to do business with God and to commit themselves to godliness, discipleship, and interpersonal reconciliation in response to the Holy Spirit's call. I'd come to Boulder to listen and to learn, but I found myself above all moved to worship.

Several scenes had imprinted themselves in my memory

as for two days I watched over fifty thousand men sing, play, learn, and worship together. There was, for example, the spectacle of hundreds of men coming forward Friday night to accept God's gift of salvation in Christ, flowing like a river from every tier in the stadium, welcomed into God's family with a thunderous ovation. I remembered, too, the Saturday morning huddle groups, men confiding their struggles to one another and praying with what one woman described as a groan. "I could hear their pain," she said, "and I couldn't help but weep." And throughout the rest of that day as the speakers instructed, encouraged, challenged, and sometimes cried before God's sons, I'd watched men's eyes and searched their faces and felt God's Spirit stirring among them.

On that final evening, my tears blurring my vision as the men abandoned themselves to worship in the deepening shadows of the Colorado nightfall, a tenderness arose in me I could hardly contain, a joy and compassion and sorrow for the wonderful strength and crushing weakness in them all. They were men. Just men. But men who were tasting God's Spirit, some of them for the first time, some of them more deeply than ever before, many of them in a whole new way. Caught up in the wonder of God's Presence, together we worshiped—fifty-three thousand men and I—at the throne of our glorious God.

DIVINE REVEILLE

Later, toward the end of that night's meeting, Bill McCartney asked the men gathered in Folsom Stadium two piercing questions: *What is God doing here? How are we going to respond?*

What God was doing at that conference—and has been doing in many other arenas of spiritual awakening as well—was issuing a "wake-up call" to His men, sending His Spirit to quicken their hearts, inviting them to yield their lives to Him, and giving them assurance that their spiritual "engines" could run. This was God's divine reveille, summoning men to a passionate involvement with Himself so they could participate in His holy agenda for drawing women, children, and other men to the refreshment of His heart of love.

But that conference and others like it, as exciting and life-altering as they are, represent only the beginning of what will likely be an ongoing process of change for the men who attend them. God's sons, convened in that Boulder stadium on that Saturday night in July, went home the next day to their wives, families, friends, jobs, neighborhoods, and churches. They also went back to the same challenges, temptations, and habits of thinking and doing that had already been in place for many years.

And that reality highlighted the importance of Bill McCartney's second question: *How are we going to respond?* The men listening to him confronted that question in their own hearts before God, but their answers would not remain a secret. They would live out those answers by the changes they would make in their everyday lives, particularly in their relationships. The interpersonal connectedness of those men to God and others is where the life-altering work of the Holy Spirit in their hearts would be most evident in the coming weeks and years.

RENEWED RELATIONSHIPS

"Given the loss of the father in the lives of so many men, it's no wonder the majority of men in the Church today feel relationally flattened," declared author Ron Ross to participants at the 1993 Florida Networking Conference in Titusville, Florida. Someone else said it this way: "Isolation is a key problem facing men throughout our culture." Confused and often frustrated by a perceived sense of relational inadequacy, many men have either avoided deeply meaningful relationships altogether, or they have approached them deflated. They may be going through the motions of connecting with the important people in their lives, but the connections often feel hollow and merely behavioral. The fact that many of them had little or no heart-connection with a loving father is one reason they live isolated as adult men. Who was there to model for them how to venture beyond the shallows in their interactions with others, including God?

Nevertheless, when God calls men to a living relationship with Himself, He is not willing to leave men flattened. His divine Father-heart longs to draw His sons into close fellowship, reconciling them to Himself through the gospel of His Son (2 Corinthians 5:18-21). He then intends to send them out as His ambassadors, commissioning them to live out His image in them through their involvement and aliveness in relating to others, especially their wives and children. In fact, the fundamental message of the call to integrity issued at the Promise Keepers conference I attended was for sons of God to become vehicles of God's grace in all their relationships—with family, friends, coworkers, pastors, men of other races and denominations, and the unchurched.

But Bill McCartney's question is for us women, too: How are we going to respond to the fact that God intends to send His sons to us as ambassadors of His grace and kindness? How will we receive them? What will be our reaction to the changes we see in them? What will we do with God Himself?

We as Christian women have always wanted men to be present to our hearts, cherishing us and caring for us as God meant them to do on His behalf. And if we haven't experienced that from men, some of us have not known to grieve the loss. Instead, we have sometimes decided to want less from men, deadening our desire and turning our attention to other people and projects to satiate our appetite for connectedness. We have masked our loneliness and cloaked our passion, because asking our fathers or husbands for their kind involvement might make us feel needy or foolish.

Thus, even if men attend a conference or seminar and come back eager to let God into their lives, we may be afraid to hope again, afraid to trust their enthusiastic words, afraid their spiritual awakening won't last beyond a few weeks or months. And the enemy of our souls will be vigilant to turn our fear into cynicism at the first indication that our men, though changed, are not yet without their faults.

The problem, however, lies deeper than our distrust of the changes we may see in the men God is drawing to spiritual renewal. We must also think about what it will cost us if men embrace spiritual aliveness. If they come alive, it will invite us to enter a responsive and reciprocal aliveness in ourselves as well—both toward them and toward God. Change always has a ripple effect, and God's intent may be to use men's spiritual awakening to draw us into greater intimacy with Himself as well. His Spirit may call us to face both our desire for and our disappointment with men, taking a closer look at what lies deep within our own hearts. Our challenge then will be to explore with integrity what we find in those hearts—toward men, toward ourselves, and especially toward God. And because all change—even good change—is disruptive, we can expect our relational boats to be rocked.

OUR CALL TO RESPONSIVENESS
Some women, for example, have experienced damage at the hands of men. Over the years of my ministry to women I've talked with many who are struggling to respond with openness to men they feel are not or have not been "there" for them. To them and to all of us, God's call is to explore what it means to live in our male-female relationships with integrity and courage as God's beloved daughters.

Our challenge goes beyond recognizing that men are changing and so can we. It means that regardless of whether men change or not, God desires that we respond to His passionate love for us and ponder how we can live as female image-bearers of the Triune God. We must ask questions not just about who men are and who they are becoming, but who we are as women and what we long to receive from God and from men.

The questions may be unsettling. Our journey into hope could bring us face to face with how men have alternately blessed and disappointed us, and we may have to grapple with how to live without giving way to fear in the midst of both realities. Some of us must choose whether to follow the trail of our relational discontent into sorrow, instead of pretending we don't care about men's hearts, or settling for polishing our performance as daughters or wives. And we may need to search both our own hearts and God's Word to discover what is most deeply true about ourselves as women.

Thus, this book will address three fundamental questions: What does Scripture teach regarding God's design for His image-bearers, male and female? If we have been disappointed with men, what can we do to move into a willingness to live with integrity and kindness before them? What would it look like to cooperate with God's design by living as His daughters in intimate relationship with Him and with good men?

Just as Bill McCartney invited those fifty-three thousand men in Boulder to come alive to the Holy Spirit's stirring of their hearts, so we are called as women of integrity to trust God's goodness and to respond to good men, receiving them as God receives us all when we come—with joyous welcome and an abundance of hope and a dogged commitment to persevere in courageous love. As we abandon ourselves more and more to the embrace of His Father-love, we can come to know ourselves deeply cherished, and we will taste what it means to find rest for our souls.

Will this journey be easy? Of course not. How soon will it be over? It will take a lifetime. How will we find the courage to do what we must? We will desperately need God. Will the end result be worth the cost? Nothing more nourishes our feminine hearts than moving to the mystery of the dance of love.

Come, let us draw near to the heart of God and talk heart to heart about men.

PART ONE

Embracing God's Design

CHAPTER ONE

OUR UNQUENCHABLE DESIRE: AFFIRMING GOD'S DESIGN

*Feminine is good and masculine is good,
and both together are even better.*
LUCI SHAW

Annemarie and I sat across from each other in the half-empty restaurant and talked over breakfast. She was twenty-one, the daughter of dear friends, and I had a few questions I wanted to ask her.

"What do you think a woman most longs to receive from a man?" I began.

After a thoughtful pause, she replied with a firm nod, "His heart."

"And what do you think a man most longs to give to a woman?" I also wanted to know.

"Not his heart," she answered, without hesitation.

"Why not?" I pursued.

"Because he knows if he gives his heart he's done for. He can't take it back."

Quite an insight from so young a woman, I thought.

WOMEN'S HEARTS TOWARD MEN

Our feminine hearts do desire men's hearts turned toward us, delighting in our beauty and cherishing who we are. We want to be wanted by them in ways that will reflect God's longing for His people and Christ's yearning to bless His Church.

It's not that men don't *want* to give their hearts to us. My sister, Peg De Boer, accurately observed, "Men probably love us more deeply than we are able to believe." But some men fear how out-of-control things will seem if they admit how much they do long for connectedness with us. To desire us as Christ desires His Church will require what seems to be their very death.

However, Annemarie also put words to what we as women deeply fear—that our longing for men's hearts will be unmet and our love for them will go unrequited. Some women who have given up hope of ever being loved as they once dreamed of being loved may settle for men's gifts of acquisition, reputation, or compliance. But what we most deeply desire is more of men's hearts, not more of what they earn or do. One woman said, "We often have the presence of men's bodies, but nothing can substitute for the presence of their hearts. What we value most is not their competence but their blessing. The Samaritan woman at the well asked Jesus for water, but He gave her His heart."

Who can unravel the mystery of a woman's heart toward men? In the stories women have been telling me for over thirty years and in my interviews with over twenty-five Christian women from across North America as I prepared to write this book, I have listened to the hearts of countless women— their hopes and dreams, their joys and sorrows, their hunger for God, and their struggles to love others wisely and well. They have been at all stages of the journey in their relationships with men, and no two stories have been alike.

I have heard women's stories about fathers enjoying the hearts of their daughters, husbands being lovingly involved with their wives, and men using their strength to protect women and children from damage or harm. As I watched the faces of those women who had been blessed by men, my heart was drawn to celebrate with them the goodness of God's provision.

But I have also heard tales of women grieving the death of their relationships with men—stories of singles used and discarded by men who defrauded them, wives young and old deserted by their mates, women of lost hope who had attached themselves to men addicted to alcohol or drugs or work or sex, women living in marriages of stark loneliness because their husbands are there but not there, having made themselves emotionally or spiritually unavailable. I have seen the pain in those women's eyes and have heard the disappointment in their voices and have tasted the anger that leaked from underneath their words. Sometimes they themselves did not recognize how much more of men's hearts they wanted than they were experiencing. A few had lost their way, shaken loose from their spiritual moorings by upheaval in their lives. Many more had not perceived the nobility and integrity of their own tenacious struggle to keep on believing in God's goodness, even in the context of their losses.

And as I listened to and sometimes probed beneath the stories women have told me about their relationships with men, I tasted the dignity and courageous faith behind the difficult questions many were asking—questions with which we all struggle from time to time: How do we face our relational disappointments without giving up? Is it wrong to try to get men to change? How does God expect us to bless men even when they are not blessing us? And is He cruel to design us to want more than we'll ever get this side of Heaven?

These are the thorny questions only a woman of integrity dares ask of her own heart. Many women I have known have grappled valiantly with the dilemma posed by such questions, each in her own way, each with her own story, each within the context of her relationship with God. These women of faith offered no easy answers, no static codes, no remedies. But they were not afraid to struggle, and in that they are models for us all.

Though every woman is as unique as her own story, we sometimes best understand and interpret our own stories by listening to each other. However, our final point of reference must reach beyond both our own experiences and the collective experiences of other women. What is most fundamentally true about the hearts of women is revealed in the pages of Scripture. Not only can we learn from watching God's people as they relate to one another as men and women, but we also find God Himself modeling how we are to be in our relationships through His own pursuit of and intimacy with His people.

Thus, if we are to understand who we are as women, we must attend to what God has to say in His Word. Perhaps the beginning is as good a place as any to start.

DESIGNED FOR RELATIONSHIP

"In the beginning, God created the heavens and the earth" (Genesis 1:1). God took what was formless, empty, and dark, and His Spirit brooded until His Word called a universe into being and shape. Twenty-five verses tell the story.

But an interesting shift occurs in the twenty-sixth verse. Instead of God speaking the Word into the void to call forth order and being out of chaos, we overhear God speaking within and to Himself: "Then God said, 'Let us make man in our image, in our likeness'" (Genesis 1:26). It is our first scriptural clue that God, though singular, exists in a plurality of Personhood. He is a social being, three Persons in One God, unity in Trinity.

When God created man in His own image, He intended male and female to reflect the society within the Godhead, the man to move as wooer, the woman to respond with gladness, both of them together to cooperate with God in bringing new life out of love. Whatever the incomprehensible intricacies of relationship within the Godhead might be, men and women in their union experience and evidence God's nature, revealing to each other and to a watching world what God is essentially like in His glad give and take of love.

In the second chapter of Genesis we learn that God made the man before He made the woman, giving him a home, food, a job, and a moral code. Then we read these startling words: "The LORD God said, 'It is not good for the man to be alone'" (2:18). Without another human being to complete or fill in the empty space in him, this man did not adequately image the essentially relational nature of God— the dynamic, joyous, intimate love relationship among Father, Son, and Holy Spirit.

So God determined, "I will make a helper suitable for him" (2:18). And what God drew out of the man and shaped according to His creative design, then brought to him to benefit him and add brightness and depth to his existence was not another man, but a woman (2:21-22). God's image-bearers were now male and female—God's final and perhaps His most wonderful act of creation.

Consider some details of God's separation of a rib from the man to form the woman who would counteract his aloneness. For example, God had spoken into being an entire universe, animate and inanimate, with His all-powerful Word. But in creating human beings, He was much more intimate. He personally "formed the man from the dust of the ground" into a being who would somehow reflect in his flesh who God was as a spirit (2:7). He also did more than speak the woman into existence. Rather, He "caused the man to fall into a deep sleep; and while he was sleeping, he took one of the man's ribs and closed up the place with flesh. Then the LORD God made a woman from the rib he had taken out of the man, and he brought her to the man" (2:21). Nothing else in creation was so deliberately brought forth from the hands of God.

It also seems significant that God put the man into a deep sleep while He formed a helper suitable for him. It was not man's human initiation but God's that brought the woman into being. The man's contribution was his "death," his deep sleep. He had to "die" and suffer the loss of an intrinsic part of himself for God to bring the woman to life, setting the pattern the Apostle Paul would later describe in Ephesians 5 as a husband's sacrificial love. How true that the man, in loving his wife, would love his own self, as Paul also says in Ephesians 5. She was formed of his bone and flesh;

there was something of him in her, though she was distinct from him and owed her being to God alone.

Note, also, that God took care to be the One with whom both the man and the woman would first experience personal relationship. Created to relate, their first taste of relationship was with Him. The man was alone with God for some time, hearing His law, enjoying His fellowship, doing the tasks God had set before him. And the woman was with God while the man slept, communing with Him alone until He brought her to the man. The One each first laid eyes on was God, and the set of their hearts' sail was instantly and irrevocably toward Him. The man was devoted to God before he even knew he needed a wife, and when God brought her to him, he had no trouble distinguishing between the gift and the Giver. The woman, too, experienced personal relationship with God before she even knew there was a man for her to bless and help. Her responsiveness to God's delight in her must surely have prepared her to receive her husband's elation at her coming.

Why would God take care to connect individually with the man and with the woman before He brought them together? Perhaps they needed the imprint of God's face to be their maiden experience of the heart-to-heart connection they were created to receive and give. And out of the overflow of that primordial love connection with God they found the pattern and energy for joyously giving themselves in love to each other.

The initial adoration of our first parents toward their Creator enhanced their love for one another as His creatures. God never intended to compete with men for the devotion of women, nor with women for the delight of men. Our first and greatest need as both men and women has always been connection with the heart of God. There and only there do we find the courage and selflessness to bring our hearts to one another.

THE DELIGHT OF DIVERSITY
The divine sexual differentiation in God's fashioning of woman for man marvelously reflects the Trinity's own passion for unity in diversity. Intimately and indivisibly One, God is nonetheless revealed as Three distinct, divine Persons. The Father is neither the Son nor the Holy Spirit. More than that, the Father did not leave Heaven to be incarnate by the virgin Mary, nor did the Son appear in what seemed like tongues of fire to fill the hearts of the disciples on Pentecost, nor does the Holy Spirit set the time of Christ's return in glory. Each distinct Person of the Trinity fulfills what is mutually and "unanimously" decreed for that Person's unique contribution in carrying out the eternal loving purposes of God. This is the unspeakable mystery of unity in diversity within the Godhead.

And that is what we reflect—though not fully, of course—as male and female image-bearers of God. When God brought the woman to the man, he recognized instantly both her likeness to him ("This is now bone of my bones and flesh of my flesh") and her uniqueness from him ("she shall be called 'woman,' for she was taken out of man"—Genesis 2:23). The man and the woman were *like*, yet also delightfully *unlike* one another.

The unlikeness between men and women goes deeper than anatomy. And it seems to show up most clearly in the dissimilar perspectives we each have regarding how to be in our relationships. For example, my friend, Rachael Crabb, an author and conference speaker from Morrison, Colorado, said to me, "Men can spend an entire weekend hunting together and when you ask them what they talked about, they say, 'Hunting.'"

She shook her head and went on, "There is no way on God's green earth that two women would go away for a weekend and talk about one subject. It's just not in us."

Cinny Hicks, an author friend of mine from Philadelphia, made this comment: "God has such a sense of humor. He could not have made men and women more different in the way we relate. Little boys, for example, show they like each other by pushing and shoving and hitting. *He's my friend so I knock him across the cafeteria.* Little girls hold hands and are sweet.

"I think God made us different," she added, "because He means to throw us into complete dependency on Him; we can't come together apart from His grace."

Cinny was right. And it surely *is* God's design that we come together as men and women. God was clearly intentional about His creation of sexuality: He brought His female image-bearer to His male image-bearer for the purpose of inviting them to union. And despite their differences—in fact, because of their differences—our first parents responded without hesitation to their inherent passion for oneness. Wonderfully, they experienced unhindered and uninhibited that God-ordained desire for connectedness: "The man and his wife were both naked, and they felt no shame" (2:25). Unity danced with abandon in the presence of diversity. It is the dance every human heart longs to join.

The reason we as women desire connectedness with men (even though for varying reasons some of us may have tried to deaden that desire) is this: God designed us to find rich satisfaction for our feminine hearts as we interact with and respond to men. It is more than a desire to receive men physically. It is even more than wanting to enhance men's lives by bringing them gladness in their maleness. It is a yearning to reflect God's nature through our responsiveness to the strength men bring to us—a reflection of the dynamic giving and receiving of joyous love within the Trinity.

THE WOMAN ALONE
This feminine longing for men is a source of consternation for some women, particularly single women and women living in unhappy marriages. Contemporary society sends two messages to the woman alone, neither one biblical. *Don't need men—you're a fool to long for them,* is one wrong message. But equally untrue is the sentiment (often hinted at in

the church especially), *You're nothing without a man.* Both extremes are lies.

It's not true, on the one hand, that women are fools to admit they need men. Jane Berry, founder and president of the Institute for Urban Girls and Women in Atlanta, described the challenge of her ministry by saying: "Many young girls in the African-American community are being told not to expect anything from men—that men will only complicate their lives and hold them back. But we teach girls that even if men aren't doing all they should, we can still hold manhood in high esteem. Maleness and femaleness are from God, and it's important we go back to relating properly to our men." Jane's words are applicable in every segment of today's culture. Women who have experienced the vacancy or unkindness of men often feel driven to self-sufficiency, but making our lives work without men is surely not God's best for us.

I once sat beside an attractive young woman on an airplane, and as we chatted, I noticed on her left hand an unusual ring. Upon closer examination, however, I realized my mistake; what I'd thought was a ring was really a tattoo of a small rose, its tendrils wrapped around her finger to replicate a ring.

When I asked her about it, she told me that prior to becoming a Christian, she had committed herself to never being married because she didn't think she could ever trust a man. The tattoo on her left hand was a "wedding ring" symbolizing her marriage to herself.

I was stunned. Never had I seen so blatantly expressed the fear we often have as women that no one but ourselves will consistently "be there" for us. Most of the women of my acquaintance at least wanted to trust men; this young woman had closed her heart against trusting any but herself. Self-wedded, she had bent her energy toward doing for herself what men are designed and called to do for women, and she found herself unable to rest with either God or men.

Surely, single women can find satisfaction in their jobs

and relationships without being married, and wives unhappy with their mates must struggle to move beyond self-pity and indifference. But competence in a job or happiness in feminine friendships may not replace women's longing for connectedness with men. Women called to the single life can set their hearts toward seeking and enjoying relationships with godly men, even while (as the Apostle Paul says) "[their] aim is to be devoted to the Lord in both body and spirit" (1 Corinthians 7:34). Their aloneness, if they choose, can lead them to find connection and strength in God, which in turn will lead them to bless the lives of men as well.

For some, however, it is not an easy choice. Leanne Payne, who heads a ministry of spiritual renewal through healing prayer, said, "It's more difficult to be one person than to be a couple, listening to God together, because one grounds the other in the earthy. When I come home alone after seeing God do incredible things through my ministry, there's nothing to ground myself in, so I have to work to keep a proper balance in my life. In many ways I am unprotected, and I've had to be strong in ways I shouldn't have had to be." Without diminishing her competence to do what God has called her to do, Leanne put words to the single woman's challenge to remain alive both to her need for protection and to the sadness of having to be strong in ways God never intended for her as a woman.

At the other end of the spectrum, however, it is also not true that an unmarried woman is nothing without a man. This is a wicked twisting of the biblical truth that we as women are created for connectedness with men. In fact, it is this very lie that keeps some married women unwilling to act boldly and lovingly in their relationships with physically abusive or adulterous men. Abused or abandoned women too often allow their husbands to continue unchallenged in the sin that endangers both their feminine bodies and men's own masculine souls, instead of loving them enough to risk being alone if those men do not repent. It is not true that a woman is nothing without a man.

Our innate desire for men does not mean we're worthless if we aren't wives or mothers. It simply means we are designed for more than any of us —married or single—will experience in a fallen world. We cannot as women *make* men come to us. But we must not believe the enemy's lie that our value is determined by our connectedness to a man.

The truth is, we as God's image-bearers are whole and valued persons because we are loved by Him and can never lose that love. Therefore, because our substance as women is rooted in God's love, we do not need a husband who loves us in order to respond to God's call to love others. It is right that we long to have a man bring us God's love in the masculine voice; God knew that in our finiteness, in our being bound by our flesh and by our humanity, we would need and respond to men showing us love on His behalf. Thus, our longings are legitimate, though we must wait on God to bring whatever gifts He thinks best for us and on His timetable.

Nevertheless, having been designed to be most fully responsive in the presence of men, some women—married and single—experience great sorrow in being alone. Even as they rest in their worth in God's sight, they may also have to grieve their aloneness. And their greatest challenge will be not only to keep themselves from meeting their legitimate needs in illegitimate or immoral ways, but also to refuse to deaden their longing for men in order to avoid or alleviate their sorrow. This sorrow, in fact, is where God comes to us as women to reassure us of His love and of His treasuring of our hearts. *That* is our hope. To the extent we try to kill or suppress our desire for good men (that is, men who will image God to us and with us), we veil the patient, responsive image of God in us, because He waits with long-suffering as He invites us to intimacy with Himself.

This is mystery indeed. I do not understand it, but I know it to be true. Women (unless we've been damaged) long to relate and respond to men because that's who we are created to be. We are made to bless and help men because neither they nor we by ourselves image God accurately. Barbara Fletcher, pastor of women's ministries at Salem Alliance Church in Salem, Oregon, rightly observed, "God created women to complement men because they need us and we need them." Whether single or married, we as human beings most nearly showcase God's Triune nature as we move and respond, male and female, in loving relationship with one another's hearts. This I know from the scriptural account of creation regarding the bent of a woman's heart.

A WOMAN'S YEARNING TO BE LOVED

This, too, I know from Scripture, from the Apostle Paul's New Testament words to the Ephesian Christians: Women, both married and single, long to have men bring them their hearts by loving them sacrificially and by protecting and cherishing them. "Husbands, love your wives," Paul wrote, "just as Christ loved the church and gave himself up for her" (5:25). Men are called to lay down their lives for the sake of drawing their wives to their hearts and making them radiant with the knowledge of being loved.

"[Husbands] ought to love their wives as their own bodies," Paul went on to say, adding that "no one ever hated his own body, but he feeds and cares for it, just as Christ does the church—for we are members of his body" (5:28-30). This is what we women want men to do. We long for their nourishment, their protection, and their delight. We desire the nourishment they bring—not just food to refresh our bodies, but also words to settle our souls and affection to warm our hearts and prayers to sustain our spirits. We want them to care for us by offering us protection from danger to our lives or damage to our hearts or assaults against our dignity. And most of all, we yearn for them to delight in us, to hold us in tender esteem because they treasure who we are. We long for their eyes on our faces, their hearts connected both to us and to their own feelings toward us, their words conveying how *present* they are to who we most deeply are and how they feel about our beauty.

Pat Palau, wife of evangelist Luis Palau, talked about her desire for her husband's loving care and tender protection. "Luis has been gone for three weeks," she told me, "and he's coming home on Monday. I want him home. I want to run things past him and have him say, 'It's okay. We'll find a way.'

"Some women might say, 'You weakling, what's the matter with you?'" Pat acknowledged. "But I've lived most of my married life by myself because of Luis's traveling. And I don't think wanting his presence and his protection makes me a weak individual. I think his protection gives me a platform to be strong."

Single women no less than married women desire masculine protection and kindness, though men who are not their husbands cannot offer those things to them in the same way they do to their wives. The absence of a good man in the life of a single woman is keenly felt. Karen Lee-Thorp, an author and editor living in Glendora, California, said, "It's not that I was incapable of taking care of myself; I used to shovel the snow from my driveway in Colorado. But it's the emotional thing that happens inside a woman that says, 'I am alone and unprotected when there is no man there for me.' Covering is what we want, the sense of being enfolded and safe."

A man's sacrificial love is practically irresistible to us as women, just as Jesus' passion for our hearts draws us compellingly to Himself. Persistent, dogged love defuses even our disappointment and anger toward men if we as women are willing to receive that love. Pamela Reeve, associate professor at Multnomah Biblical Seminary in Portland, Oregon, relates this telling story:

"Back in May of 1973," Pamela said, "I attended a conference sponsored by Denver Conservative Baptist Seminary to explore one of the most volatile issues of that day: Women's role and status. The purpose of the conference was to examine from an evangelical perspective the changing role of women. Position papers were presented at various times, and each presentation was followed by a response from the opposite position.

"As the days wore on, the debate grew sharper. On the final morning of the conference, then-Professor Kermit Ecklebarger taught from Ephesians 5, emphasizing that a husband's leadership should be selfless and respectful of his wife's strengths, insights, and abilities.

"When he finished," Pamela recalled, "Dr. Virginia Mollenkott rose to her feet to respond, and I fully expected the usual strong rebuttal. Instead, she was visibly moved, saying, 'If men would treat us like that, there would be no need for meetings such as these.'"

Dr. Mollenkott's words ring true. In the presence of masculine kindness and cherishing we find ourselves invited to open our hearts to men. We are, in fact, designed to respond to their sacrificial love and heartfelt esteem.

HEART-TO-HEART CHERISHING

Every woman longs to be cherished, to be affirmed for her inner beauty. Yet few women believe themselves beautiful enough to be deeply valued. Our culture's emphasis on youth and sex appeal has hindered many women from embracing the beauty of their hearts—the inner beauty God sees and in which He delights. Yet in spite of ourselves, we women yearn for men to cherish us as Christ treasures the Church, even when we feel unlovely. *Especially* when we feel unlovely.

A recent article in *Discipleship Journal* describes a man who cherished his wife. Joyce Clayton Morse tells the story.

He was seventy-six and she was sixty-six when the stroke took away her ability to walk, talk, read, write, cook, sew, paint, teach Sunday school, and be everyone's "calm voice of reason" in the storm.

Two weeks after they told him their long-term goal for her was to be able to turn herself over in bed, he stopped eating. This man fasted and prayed for ten days. No one else knew—not even her.

When she checked out of the rehab center a

month later, she could walk three hundred feet with a hemi-walker and dress and undress herself with little help.

In the next fifteen months, he learned to cook (and find the best take-outs in town), to check her blood sugar, to pay the bills and balance the checkbook, and to keep her appointments straight. You should have seen those strong, work-worn, mechanic's fingers tenderly combing her hair and fixing it in the ponytail style he devised. When they told him he needed surgery for lung cancer, he said that if he could just have "one more good year" to help her get better, he wouldn't bother with the surgery.

One night in CCU, they took a portable phone to his bed and he spoke with her one last time. "Sugar," he said, "I'm thinking about you all the time. I can't wait to be home with you. I love you and it's going to be all right." His pain-ravaged face was incandescent with love. She said the only word the stroke had left her, "no, no, no, no," but he heard her meaning.

Grown men stood and wept uncontrollably at his graveside. Women wondered if their men would stand by them with that kind of sacrificial love. That gentle, enduring love wasn't a new idea to him, though—he learned it from his Father. I learned it from mine.[1]

Some of us cannot believe a man would love us that sacrificially nor cherish our hearts as this man so obviously cherished his wife's heart, even when her body was crippled by stroke. Some of us have had little experience in our families or churches of men who treasured our hearts despite our shortcomings, and we have concluded we are unlovely. But that does not mitigate our hunger to be treasured. That longing and the hope that it will be met have flowered at one time or another in every feminine soul.

This longing, in fact, reflects the very image of God in us, because He is not neutral regarding us. He is passionate for our hearts and will stop at nothing to win us to Himself. Relationship is central to His nature and central to His gospel of reconciliation. That is why we, as His image-bearers, are passionate for one another's hearts, particularly as men and women. My sister Mary Swierenga rightly said, "As God yearns for us to love Him, so we yearn for another to love us. We long to know and be known, yet still and always to be accepted."

This, above all, I know to be true of the hearts of women: What we long to receive from a man is his enraptured heart, reflecting what we have tasted as daughters restored to our heavenly Father because of Calvary—the delight in His eyes as He looks on our face. The struggle comes if our feminine hearts are not tasting from men the love God designed us to receive. The next chapters will explore the impact of what we have done with that loss and the hope that comes when we invite God into the loss with us.

In the belief that God was being both wise and good when He created us to long for and respond to men, may we grow in the grace required to receive (or perhaps wait to receive) what we most deeply desire: the coming of God and the coming of good men to our hearts.

QUESTIONS FOR REFLECTION AND DISCUSSION
This closing section at the end of each chapter poses questions that invite you to consider what shifts in your attitudes and behavior toward men you are willing to make in response to God's coming to you. We cannot change men. In fact, we cannot even change ourselves. We can only put ourselves in the presence of and under the mercy of the One who alone can refashion our hearts. We do that when we quiet our souls, take our courage in hand, and face our inner lives in the presence of God's kind but unflinching gaze. Ponder, journal, and discuss your thoughts regarding these soul-searching questions.

1. If the men in your life have blessed you, are you remembering to be grateful?
2. Are you willing to stop demanding more from them?
3. If you have not been blessed by men, how are you moving toward becoming able to forgive men?
4. In what ways do you struggle to embrace God's design for you as a woman?
5. What might it look like to depend more on Scripture than on our culture to define who you are and how you are to live as a woman?
6. Do you delight in your differentness from men?
7. How can you esteem men and show them honor?
8. In what situations do you see in your heart a commitment to be "married to yourself"?
9. What things do you insist on doing for yourself that you could be asking men to do for you?
10. How can you enter your longing for connectedness with men, despite the pain of wanting more than you're receiving?

CHAPTER TWO

OUR SURVIVAL DEVICES:
DISTORTING GOD'S DESIGN

*A woman will do whatever she can to control
a man, but if she succeeds, she won't be happy.*
SUSAN YATES

I was the speaker at a women's retreat some time ago, and a young woman had asked to talk privately with me. We sat together on the beach, mostly alone, and I shed tears with this woman, whose name I cannot remember but whose face I cannot forget. Her husband, a pastor, was unwilling to seek help to break a pattern of compulsive pornography use, and she felt not just abandoned by him, but without resources herself because of her position as pastor's wife.

Though not at all unusual (I hear many such stories), this woman's words wrenched my heart. I struggled for words to encourage her honest sojourn with God and with her husband. Inwardly, however, I was furious.

My anger was not just toward her husband, who was doing sore damage to the heart of the wife he had vowed to protect. I was even more enraged at the adversary of our souls, whose energy is ever bent on destroying all who would belong to God. God's creation was perfect once, but His enemy maliciously determined to mar perfection, and his evil plan succeeded. How I hate the story! It is found in Genesis 3.

LOSS OF INTIMACY

Sadly, our first parents' perfect God-imaging did not outlast their own generation. The serpent, indwelt by God's enemy, tempted the woman to move out from under God's covering by eating forbidden fruit. Satan promised her, "[When] you eat of it your eyes will be opened, and you will be like God, knowing good and evil" (Genesis 3:5). The woman believed that achieving goddess status would satisfy her soul, not realizing that "knowing good and evil" would be a curse, not a blessing. She was deceived.

But the man was not. Scripture tells us that "Adam was not the one deceived; it was the woman who was deceived . . ." (1 Timothy 2:14). She was fooled into stepping out of God's will, but her husband, "who was with her" (3:6) during the seduction, though undeceived, did nothing. He did not draw her aside and remind her of God's goodness and the wisdom of His kind boundaries. He offered her no masculine words to woo her back to trust in God. Instead, he followed her in her disobedience, knowing clearly what he was doing, rather than pleading with God on her behalf for His poured-out mercy. Whatever else can be said about his delinquency in keeping Eden from evil, his choice to follow his wife's lead was a failure to love and protect her. She abandoned both him and God, and he did not do battle for her soul.

After their sin, our first parents concealed themselves behind the leaves of the trees that had once nourished them. How closely we, their children, resemble them in the hiding of our hearts. We attempt to live as though the damage caused by our sin is minimal or reversible by our efforts to conceal it.

Then God in His mercy came to them, though they had gone out from Him. When He called to the man, "Where are you?" it was not because God lacked the necessary data regarding the man's whereabouts. It was the man who did not know where he was. God's questions to us are never meant to enlighten Him about us, but to teach us something about our own hearts toward Him, as well as something about His own character.

The man's response to God's invitation to self-disclose was this: He admitted he was afraid and so he had hidden. Distrusting the loving heart of his Father-God, he had concealed his heart rather than ask for mercy. He chose to blame his wife instead of repent, and in his refusal to be broken by his sin, he did great damage. His upraised fist toward God and his hardened heart toward the woman wounded not only God's heart, but his own and hers as well. The man who had heretofore only delighted in his wife now turned on her in order to protect himself.

And what did she do with her heart-soreness at her husband's betrayal? How did she bear this unforeseen consequence of her goddess-lust? When God turned to her and invited her to confession as He had invited the man, she, like her husband, could have entered brokenness and pled for mercy. But she, too, hid behind blame. Concealing her heartbreak at her husband's abandonment, she aimed her accusation at the serpent. She put no words to her shame nor her sorrow at having lost intimacy with both her husband and her Lord. What was most deeply true she left unsaid, swallowing her tears and her words. We are more her daughters than we know.

And so Adam and Eve were mutually dismayed. Cut off from the heart of God, the Source of their lives, their hearts were dead to Him and to each other. They would need Another's death to restore them to relational life, and what they had before known in fullness of love they would henceforth know only in tastes until they would pass through the physical death they deserved and come Home at last. Their disobedience had cast them out of their Garden intimacy and into perpetual animosity toward God and one another, and nothing in male-female relationships has been the same since.

Our relationships as men and women must be seen against this larger backdrop of God's design: Both male and female are created to long for unbroken connection with God and with one another, but because of the Fall, we can neither love nor be loved perfectly this side of Heaven. Our loss has been monumental.

Our deepest loss, of course, is the loss of intimacy with God. We cannot know except in inklings the unhindered fellowship our first parents enjoyed with Him in their pre-Fall worship. God moves to awaken His children's hunger for Himself, but the banquet is for later, not now. It is a most arduous waiting.

We must also, on a daily basis, confront our other loss— intimacy with one another, particularly between men and women. We must all endure the consequences of the Fall, living as broken people in a broken world. We may wish it were not so. We may strive to change our circumstances or our spouses or even, somehow, our past. But we cannot undo the damage. We must face the truth that we live in an innately fallen world. We bear the scars of not having received what we were designed to desire.

WOMEN'S LOSSES

As is true for the hearts of little boys, the hearts of little girls are first damaged by their relationship (or loss of relationship) with their fathers. Less attention has been paid to the consequences of father-daughter disconnectedness than to the loss of the father-son bond, but perhaps more needs to be said. Father-deprivation is as devastating for girls as it is for boys.

My younger sister, Peg DeBoer, said this about fathers and daughters: "It's very significant for women to have proper fathering. We all as little girls want to jump on Daddy's lap and feel safe there. We want him to think we're the most wonderful thing that's happened in his whole life. I believe our sense of femininity comes from being special to Daddy." Unfortunately, many of us have not known what it is to be special to our daddies. No wonder we have difficulty believing we're special to our Father in Heaven.

What happens in the father-daughter relationship sets the stage for how a woman will relate to men later in her life. The promises a father makes to his girl-child, whether spoken or implied, teaches her about the trustworthiness of men and of God. A woman's experience with a good father does much to draw her heart toward men and toward her heavenly Father.

Dale Hanson Bourke, an author and media consultant in Washington, D.C., told me an anecdote that revealed how special she was to her father. "My father was crucial in defining who I am as a woman," she said. "Even as a grown woman, when visiting my parents on a business trip, before I'd leave for a meeting my father would stop me and say, 'Wait a minute. I just want to look at you.' Then he'd give me a hug and tell me I was a beautiful woman."

Barbara Fletcher related how she, too, felt treasured by her father. "We're at the anniversary of my father's death," Barbara told me with quiet tears, "and the loss of a father in my life has meant the loss of unconditional love. My father had Alzheimer's disease, but even when he no longer knew I was his daughter, he still knew he adored me. He lived in a care home near us, and I would see him almost every day. He'd be sitting in his chair in the lobby, and when I walked in, his face would light up like a Christmas tree—not because I looked nice or had done great things that day or had spoken at another conference, but just because he saw a face he knew he loved. I've never doubted God's love, because I received the love of my father."

Even when we don't realize it, even when we don't want to admit it, we as women long to hear the father-words, "Wait a minute. Before you go off into your busy day, I want to remind you I think you're beautiful." We're afraid to admit how parched our daughter-souls have become and how we pine for our fathers' eyes to light up when we enter a room, to be delighted to see us just because of who we are and not because of anything we've done. Tragically, too many of us have no such memories to remind us how precious we are.

For the converse is also true: A woman's experience of *not* having had a father's loving delight can set her up for further damage by men and can harden her heart against them and against God. Many women, in fact, struggle to see *father* as a positive word. One woman told me, "My father didn't make or keep promises on my behalf, so I was set up to listen to other men who would make all sorts of easy promises to me they had no intention of keeping."

Many of us have been let down in our relationships with members of the opposite sex, whether our fathers or other men. This is not to demean nor depreciate men; surely men have blessed our lives in countless ways. But being disappointed with men is intrinsic to the reality of living in a fallen world. We may have tried to minimize or forget those losses, but for some of us the wreckage of broken relationships often continues to litter our souls. And if we've hoped for more from men than they would or could give us, we've also most likely struggled to survive in the best way we know how.

The damage, of course, is always twofold. On the one hand, we have been wounded because of the sin of other people against us. Not all of us have suffered equal woundings, but none of us has been loved perfectly. On the other hand, we have also done damage to others and to ourselves by the ways we've responded not to having been loved as much as we'd hoped. We've been sinned against and we have sinned. Suffering and self-centeredness are equally inherent in the experience of us all.

WOMEN'S ANGER

We must not forget the original design: Our hearts are made to respond to men, and it's no wonder we are drawn to them. But it's also no wonder our hearts are broken when men do not come or when they leave us. Perhaps if we did not so greatly desire connection with men, we would be less angry when the connection is severed or illicit. I've heard the anger time and again, sometimes in a woman's words, often in her tone of voice, and occasionally in the words she leaves unsaid. If men have let us down, our disappointment and anger are as inevitable as our longings.

One fundamental question we must ask ourselves is what we have done with our anger, for that says much about our feminine hearts. Sometimes our disappointment turns to bitterness, which threatens to leak out despite our efforts to deny it is there. In a recent article in *Time* magazine, "Men: Are They Really That Bad?" author Lance Morrow concludes that "the overt man bashing of recent years has now . . . settled down to a vague male aversion, as if masculinity were a bad smell in the room."[1] Thus, even when we as women refrain from beating men up with our words to them or about them, in our hearts we may secretly despise them. The dilemma is particularly acute for Christian women, because we cannot justify despising anyone, not even those we feel are our enemies. What do we do with our anger?

Our disappointment if men have failed us doesn't go away just because we decide not to vent our wrath on them. Our anger is still there, even though we may struggle to deal with it in ways we think are Christian. What we often fail to realize is that what we think are "Christian" ways of dealing with our anger may not be Christ-like at all. We may have chosen self-sufficiency over stridency, passivity rather than petulance, manipulation instead of outspokenness, emotional deadness as opposed to verbal abuse. But strategies that may be more socially acceptable are not necessarily Christian. As a matter of fact, our self-sufficiency, passivity, manipulation, and deadness are neither Christ-reflective nor men-honoring. Rather, they do great damage to our own souls and to the souls of the men with whom we are in relationship. If we will listen for our heavenly Father's voice, we will discern His call to repentance—not for our anger, but for our self-destructive and other-destructive ways of dealing with that anger.

What, then, are our strategies for dealing with our

disappointment regarding men, and how do those strategies keep us from living out the image of God in us as women? In a nutshell: our refusal to live as responders in our relationships with men. Afraid we won't receive the sacrificial love we were created to respond *to*, we are tempted to shut down our hearts and squelch our desire for men. We may even kill our hope that good men will come to us, or we shame ourselves for our feminine responsiveness when good men do come. Some of us have refused to trust men's love, refused to need their protection, and refused to yearn for their cherishing. What we often don't realize, however, is that if we harden our hearts against men, we harm ourselves and them in the process.

A friend of mine once said, "Women are primarily responsive creatures, and any woman who shuts down her responsiveness loses what gives her integrity and depth as a woman." This is true not merely in the context of the marriage relationship, but for singles as well. A woman's responsiveness to men is manifest any time she receives a man's kindness with gratitude, or seeks a man's protection (on the job, for example, if such is available), or enters into her longing for the heart of a good man without coveting an illicit relationship. Sometimes it is difficult for us to live out of our feminine responsiveness, but in not running from our discomfort, we can embrace God's design for us and taste His pleasure in our willingness to live with integrity and authenticity.

Consider with me how many of us have shut down our responsiveness by distrusting men's kindness, refusing to need men's covering, and squelching our yearning for men's hearts.

RESISTANCE TO TRUST

Think first of how hard it sometimes is for us to receive men's attempts to touch our hearts with their kindness. Instead of welcoming their movement toward us, we may find ourselves demanding a guarantee of safety from any further evidence of their human frailty. We may tell them what to do or say so we won't be disappointed in what *they* want to do or say. In short, we'd rather protect ourselves than risk trusting them.

All of us emerge from our childhood with custom-designed strategies for keeping our relational lives at least moderately pain-free and somehow manageable. We've bent our energy toward doing whatever will work to keep us from sadness and in control. For many of us that means refusing to give men our hearts and instead trying to change them. Our styles may differ; some of us manage men by being door-mats, while others become tough cookies. But our agenda is the same: *Stay safe, stay strong, stay distant, stay in charge.*

One woman told me, "Because I was abused as a child, I vowed to never be dominated by a man. Of course, I've had to work through the effects of that early trauma, but I've also had to repent of my vow, because it kept me trying to control men instead of learning to be appropriately respon-sive to them.

"There has been a spirit of control in the women in our family for ten generations," she went on to say. "My grand-mother was a very competent, spiritual woman, and that is a positive. But the negative is that strong women tend to emasculate men." It is a tightrope many women walk, some with greater success than others.

Scripture calls us to respect men by trusting their hearts and asking respectfully for their kind movement toward us. But because some men have shown themselves untrust-worthy, we may struggle to trust our hearts to *any* man. Instead, we may take the lead in our male-female relation-ships and even try to teach them how to be men so they will be what we think they should be. Often we try to recreate them in our own image—to make them like our female friends who can more easily listen to our stories and empathize with our pain. We insist that men be more like women, though it's not what we *really* want. It is our fear that causes us to feminize men; we hate feeling so out of control in relating to their masculine hearts.

Implied in our distrustful attempts to change men is the assumption that we as women know best and are somehow in possession of knowledge and skills men will never acquire by themselves. I've known women who believe men are incapable of having—let alone expressing—genuine emotion about anything. How condescending toward men! Cinny Hicks was right when she said, "Our demand for radical change in our men presupposes that we women have the edge on relationships and spirituality and men need to catch up. I'm not sure that's the case." Surely many men are conditioned by their past experiences not to engage their feelings (except, perhaps, their anger), not to talk about their inner lives, and never, of course, to cry. Nevertheless, men as much as women are created with intense feelings.

Jesus, our perfect example, was a man of unquestioned masculinity and capable of a far broader range of emotions than the righteous anger He displayed when driving the money-changers from the temple courtyard (Matthew 21:12-13). He declared (perhaps with tears) that He "longed" to draw even the pharisaical prophet-killers to Himself like a mother hen gathers her young (23:37). He wept openly when His friend Lazarus died, because He loved him (John 11:35-36). Just before His crucifixion He told His disciples that He "eagerly desired" to share His last Passover meal with them (Luke 22:15). In Gethsemane He was "in anguish" (22:44), and twice from the cross He "cried out in a loud voice" (Matthew 27:46,50). Not only was Jesus in touch with what was in His heart, He was not afraid to express it in actions and in words. He offers us a clear example of what it means to be a good man, and women, too, can learn from Him how to be present to their own souls.

We do not have to teach men how to feel or what to do. They already *have* feelings (however suppressed or unacknowledged) and they have available to them the leading of the Holy Spirit to show them what to do. It is not our job to train them to image God in their relationships, though that is a soul-diminishing project we often undertake. The truth is, we women have much to learn from men about how to be in our relationships, if only we will be humble enough to listen and wait and give up trying to run their lives for them.

My friend Judy Vander Plate, a pastor's wife from Fremont, Michigan, spoke these words about her attempts to control her husband, Jack: "Years ago, when I was in great pain because I felt Jack didn't care about me, someone asked me, 'What if he never changes?' My immediate response was, 'He has to change.' That was my goal—he *had* to change. I didn't think *I* needed to change. I was running myself ragged doing all the things I thought I was supposed to be doing—and feeling pretty self-righteous about it. But now I realize that by trying to force Jack to change, I was standing in the way of what God wanted to do in him. I had to decide: Is God in charge or isn't He? And when I concluded that He was, I had to give up my control of Jack. It was hard. I'd gotten pretty good at it."

Honest words from a woman of integrity. Much like these words from my friend, Cynthia Heald, an author and seminar leader living in Tucson, Arizona, regarding her relationship with her husband (also named Jack): "I went through a time when I was trying to get Jack to be more spiritual and do what I thought he should do as the leader in our home," Cynthia told me, "and I was really frustrated because he wasn't doing those things. One day the Lord asked me, 'Are you ready to give up with Jack and release him?' And I remember saying to God, 'No, I'm not. There are a couple more things I need to do yet.'"

I laughed because I recognized myself in Cynthia's candid words, but she added, "I was dead serious about it. It was a while before I was able to say, 'Okay, God, he's yours.'"

"The best definition of submission I've ever heard," she declared, "is this: *Ducking low enough so God can touch your husband.* Once I got out of the way, God began doing incredible things in Jack's life—but not in my way nor on my timetable."

It is God who moves in men's hearts to teach them how to be in their relationships. When we try to be God's voice telling men what to do and how to do it, they can't hear what God wants to say to them. Men can dismiss our words in ways they will find it impossible to dismiss the words of the God of the universe. And how can we be sure that what God wants to say is the same as what *we* want to say?

Too often we as women try to manipulate men into doing or being what will suit us. And when we become movers and striders on our own behalf and for our own self-centered ends, we do ourselves damage. More than that, we damage men by implying, or perhaps even saying outright, *You are not the man you ought to be—let me teach you how to be more manly.* Such words from a woman's mouth or her attitude do damage to her own soul, even as they fail to respect the man to whom she communicates them.

REFUSAL TO NEED

Resistance to trust is not the only way we can fail to be responders to the hearts of men. Instead of receiving what men bring us as providers for our physical, emotional, and spiritual well-being, we women sometimes also become experts at not needing men. And when we do not receive what we were designed to want from them, we are likely to move toward toughening ourselves rather than toward sorrow. Choosing not to turn to God for comfort and cherishing as His beloved daughters, we become strong for ourselves, not realizing that our strategies for protecting ourselves do harm to our hearts. Moreover, those strategies do not bring us what our souls most deeply desire, which is intimacy and rest with God and with good men.

Don't get me wrong. I would never advocate a whiny, "I can't live without a man," kind of neediness in women. I have known too many women—myself included—who have found themselves enmeshed in an emotionally controlled and controlling relationship with the men in their lives. It is an idolatry neither pleasing to God nor attractive to men.

Nevertheless, we as women can do men great harm when we refuse to ask for or need what they can bring us—their kindness, their strength, and their delight in us. Self-sufficient independence has never been God's design for us as His daughters. It narrows the scope of our potential to bless and damages a man's sense of adequacy to love women well.

Consider these anecdotes from two women willing to be candid about their own destructive self-sufficiency in relating to men. Rachael Crabb said about her relationship with her husband: "Several years ago I asked Larry what I was doing that made him act more tenderly toward other people than toward me. And it boiled down to these words from him: 'You act like you never need me.' I think that has been my problem. I could be hurting badly, but I wouldn't give in to needing Larry because I knew I could get hurt by needing him. Men can let you down, and it's just easier to not need our husbands—or God, either—than to be hurt." Rachael's words about the connection between refusing to need men and refusing to need God are surely true, and her self-protective strategy is one that many of us have embraced at one time or another.

Penny Freeman, who teaches counseling in the graduate department at Philadelphia College of Bible, acknowledged her earlier indifference toward her husband in these words: "I think that up until the last couple of years, my job was to try to *not* need John. If you don't need anything from people and they can't do anything to add to your life, then there's certainly not a lot they can take away either. That's why our marriage was so pitiful. I had basically done an excellent job of eliminating my need for John. I think it was breaking his heart." How sad—for both men and women—when we react to men's failure to provide for our souls by refusing to long for their provision. Grieving the loss of provision is one thing; refusing to want or need it is quite another.

We so often are afraid men won't protect us from what

can do us harm. Though we are designed to be covered by the strength of good men, we sometimes think they won't do the job or won't do it well enough, and our only hope is to protect ourselves. Even if we present the external appearance of softness and femininity, some of us find ourselves inwardly tough and vigilant in our commitment not to be hurt again. We may be willing to offer our hands but not our hearts. We may even offer our bodies but not our hearts because we think the risk is too great. Victimized by our need to self-protect, our restless souls remain fearfully alone. This I have tasted time and again in the stories I have heard from women.

"I grew up feeling very distant from my father," one woman told me. "I felt I would never be a part of him nor he a part of me. My mother was his second wife, his first wife having died of cancer. He respected women, but because I didn't emotionally bond with him, I grew up with the determination, 'If I can't have your love, I will earn your respect.'

"I remember an incident that was a turning point for me," she went on to say. "My father had lost two infant sons from his first marriage, but he had a daughter who was twenty when I was born, and he just idealized her. My stepsister's term for my father was Papa; my term was Daddy. One day, when I was six or seven, I came bouncing into the house very excited and bursting with something I wanted to tell him. He was sitting in his big chair reading his paper, and I began to tell him my exciting news, expecting him to put down his paper the way he always did to give me his full attention.

"But this day I started out by exclaiming, 'Oh Papa . . . ,' and he looked at me with a look I'd never seen before nor have I since. Suddenly his eyes went cold and steely, and he turned to me and said, 'Don't ever call me that again.' And with that he turned and picked up his paper.

"I remember going off and saying to myself, 'I will never be part of him. He has a closeness with my stepsister I'm not a part of and never will be.' I was shut out, and it had come across with incredible force. I think in retrospect I determined right then I would have to make it on my own as far as he was concerned."

Did you catch this wounded woman's conclusion? "I will have to make it on my own as far as my father is concerned." When we as women refuse to need our fathers' or our husands' protection—for whatever reason, even if the reason is legitimate or good men have been unavailable—we are set up to refuse to need the protection of any man. We may be in relationships with many men and may even be married, but we will often find ourselves unable to be at rest with men or to need what they can bring us. These things we will try to provide for ourselves.

That is what happened to another woman with whom I spoke. "I remember early in our marriage when a financial crisis came along because of my husband's failure to plan well," she said. "I determined right then that if my husband wasn't going to take care of me, I would take care of myself, and I kicked into a survival mode that lasted for fifteen years. I was an angry, angry woman, and nobody has been more controlling than I have.

"But I see it all around," she continued. "I know many women who have shut off their hearts and become cold and calculating. Their tears, if they come, make them uncomfortable because it shows a soft and tender side that undermines their sense of control. Yet that tender softness is how God made us as women."

It is that very softness which is compromised when we move into toughness to protect our hearts from further damage. Because we are meant to be responders, our determined self-sufficiency—however reasonable or justified—keeps us not only from enjoying the covering men are called to provide for us, but also from resting in the assurance of God's sovereign protection of our souls.

UNWILLINGNESS TO YEARN

What wounded women are really running from, of course, is not just men, but from our *yearning* for good men. God's intention that we respond to being cherished by our fathers and by other men means that our longing for connectedness will not die. Many of us, for example, find ourselves drawn to romance novels to experience vicariously a world where men are strong and kind, reflecting our desire to receive the tenderness of a man who wants and delights in us. Even if we feel shamed by our yearning to be treasured, perhaps it's because that desire has not been affirmed nor satisfied by good men.

Unfortunately, no one taught us how to live when we didn't receive as children and young women what we were created to desire. We learned to survive, but often it was at the expense of our longings. Some of us have deadened our hearts against wanting to be treasured, because we thought it would never happen, and we thought we could not bear the loss.

However feminine our appearance or genteel the work of our hands, our eyes and our hearts have sometimes been turned aside from our yearning to be cherished. Some of us have become steel magnolias, afraid that when a man we admire sees us for who we really are, he will either use us for his own ends, or his eyes will turn away from us in disgust. We've felt the betrayal before, and because we thought we would not survive the pain, we have turned our life's energy toward somehow proving that we deserve to be cherished. With God and with men, we try to earn the delight of their hearts.

Is this not the energy behind our dogged attempts to do everything right? We drive ourselves with pharisaical determination to be good daughters, good wives, good lovers, good mothers, good homemakers, good workers, good *whatever*, so that we will see the delight we long to see in the eyes of the men we admire. We refuse to believe what my friend, author Kevin Huggins, said: "It is never a sin to ask to be loved, but it is always a sin to try to earn it."

We think it's smart to try to earn love, and we have often been rewarded for our striving. We cling to the notion that perfectionism is our ticket to paradise. We work hard and try to look good and apologize profusely—*too* profusely—for our every mistake in the hope we will finally be loved.

And when our perfectionism doesn't get us the treasuring we so desperately desire, we get mad. "You *owe* me!" we cry out to God and to men, our broken hearts obscured by our brandished fists. "I've done everything I could do, and you still aren't satisfied! See if I try anymore! I was a fool to want your cherishing in the first place!"

And so we shame our hearts, deaden our desire, and refuse to bring our hearts to God or to men. Our lives become unreal and our hearts are in danger of being seduced by illicit ways of meeting the longing for love that leaks out despite our vigilance to conceal it. Thank God, He sometimes intervenes to keep us from great harm by inviting us to sorrow over our hardened hearts.

Mary Kassian, an author and teacher residing in Edmonton, Alberta, related this compelling story: "I was speaking at a retreat once," she said, "and I had an opportunity to pray with a woman who had been raped twenty-five years earlier by an assailant she did not know. After the incident, she had just gone on with her life, going through the motions, getting married, always doing the right things, but never quite *there*. She felt like she was watching herself live life, and she had a tough, competent exterior.

"She'd never forgiven the fellow who raped her," Mary went on to say, "and though the damage he did was terrible, her response was to let layer upon layer of hardness and bitterness make her almost unable to feel and interact with her world.

"However, when we prayed together about forgiving him, something broke in this woman. She was completely shattered and fell sobbing on the floor. But when she got up, there was a light in her eyes, and she was a different woman.

"I saw her again some time later, and she said she's now *feeling* again, enjoying the sunshine and delighting in her family and able to respond to her husband.

"Sometimes the healing process takes a much longer

time," Mary concluded. "I find in my own experience it has been a journey with no magic cures. But being broken by sorrow instead of hardened by deadness is an integral part of forgiveness."

If we deaden our hearts against our desire to be valued and protected by men, we harden our hearts against God as well. We cannot be alive to Him unless we are alive to our own hearts. The Apostle Paul compares the intimate relationship between husband and wife, for example, to the mystery of Christ's relationship to the Church, and though I don't fully understand it, I know there is a connection between a woman's longing to respond to good men and the Church's willingness to desire and respond to Christ. This mystery is most precious, and our refusal to yearn locks us out of God's embrace as surely as it keeps us from the kindness of good men.

THE REVIVAL OF HOPE

Where, then, is our hope as women? Some of us have refused to be the responders we were designed to be. We hesitate to trust men, but our doing their job for them hasn't seemed right because we are, after all, women. We shrink from needing men, but our self-sufficiency has kept us from resting in the strength of a good God and good men. We are ashamed to yearn for cherishing, but deadening our souls to avoid the pain of any additional disappointment has darkened and narrowed our world to a gray existence masquerading as life.

And in forsaking our feminine responsiveness, we have become shrewish and tired. Shrewish, because demanding seems the only way to procure for ourselves what we are not getting (or not getting enough of) from the men in our lives. Tired, because we have exhausted ourselves trying to maintain both sides of our relationships with men, and we don't know if we can do it anymore.

At the deeper levels of our souls, we women know we want to do more than shut down our hearts or merely survive. We long for more in our relationships with men, even though we don't always know what "more" would look like. We have believed for too long that the ways we have been living are our only choices about how to live.

But that is not true. We can live with hope that we will receive the love for which we long, because the deep relational chasm Satan managed to create between us as men and women in Eden is not the end of the story. He cannot destroy our souls. God always has the final word, and the basis of our hope for restoration in our relationships lies in the coming of God's gospel of grace to our lives. That is the topic of the next chapter.

In the knowledge that God is the only Source of our life and the Giver of hope to all who turn to Him, may we as women face our disappointments and confess our relational devices to the Lover of our souls, listening for the Father-words our hearts long to hear: "You are a beautiful woman, the delight of My heart!"

QUESTIONS FOR REFLECTION AND DISCUSSION
The harsh reality that God's original design for men and
women has been subverted and twisted creates tough challenges for us within the context of the brokenness confronting us daily. Consider these questions as you ponder
and discuss how to become more the woman of integrity you
want to be.

1. In what ways are you personally most aware of the devastating consequences of humankind's fall into sin,
   described in Genesis 3?
2. Are you willing to call *good* God's original design that
   women respond to men's movement toward them?
   Why, or why not?
3. In what ways have your early experiences with men
   influenced what you think of men today and how you
   presently relate to them?
4. What did you do with your anger and sorrow if those
   early experiences were harmful or disappointing?
5. How have those strategies become patterns in your
   life?
6. What are some of the ways you try to control or
   change the men in your life?
7. What do you do to protect your inner life instead
   of longing for the protection and covering of God
   and men?
8. If you have, how have you deadened your soul to keep
   from yearning to be cherished?
9. In what ways can you allow God to communicate to
   you how much He cherishes you?

OUR DIVINE ROMANCER: REINSTATING GOD'S DESIGN

I think what was damaged in the Fall was not so much women's desire, but rather the way women would go about trying to get that desire met.
BARBARA FEIL

*I*t was a clear Florida morning in mid-February, and through the window of my taxiing plane I saw a vapor heart being traced in the sky, a love message for all to see. I smiled as I thought, *I hope the feeling's mutual. That's a mighty expensive valentine!*

By the time we'd been cleared for take-off, the vapor heart was broadening and fading, and it occurred to me that God's sky-written Valentine, suspended on a cross between Heaven and earth for all to see, was far more substantial and costly than this one.

There is no question about how God feels toward us. Our divine Romancer spares no expense in showing His delight in His bride. He does not try to hide His heart, nor is He reticent to declare His intentions. He has assured us that His love will never fade and that He will keep forever His covenantal vows.

God's passion to win our hearts is no secret. What is less clear is whether or not we will reciprocate in kind.

GOD'S PURSUING HEART

Perhaps the most wonderfully gracious truth about the tragic events described in Genesis 3 is that our Creator-God did not leave us without hope after Eden's disaster, self-inflicted though it was. The man and woman He had made to image His love ran from Him after their disobedience. So it was left to God to seek them out and speak of mercy—to pronounce judgment and to promise salvation and to name its cost. It was His valentine of grace.

God's glory is that He loves the unworthy, the disgraced, the disreputable, the fallen. He is under no compulsion; He loves because that is His nature. And so He came to the Garden immediately after the Fall to reveal His gracious plan for bringing His children back to His embrace. He could have turned them over to His enemy; it would have been just, given their alignment with Satan in their disobedience. But instead God declared a state of perpetual warfare, saying to the serpent, "I will put enmity between you and the woman, and between your offspring and hers; he will crush your head, and you will strike his heel" (Genesis 3:15).

This enmity between human beings and the Evil One would be played out not just between God's image-bearers and the forces of evil, but between one Man and Satan himself. The woman's "offspring" (the Hebrew word is singular), who was marked for battle with the "offspring" of Satan, is none other than Jesus of Nazareth. He would engage in mortal "hand-to-hand" combat with God's enemy. The combat would be mortal not just because it would end in Jesus' death, but because He would fight on behalf of us mortals, men and women who need a flesh-and-blood champion to represent us in the battle against evil we ourselves cannot win.

But because Jesus would be God as well as man, He could and did win that battle, as God announced in the gospel message to our first parents: The woman's offspring would suffer a strike to His heel, but He would deal a crushing, lethal blow to the head of the Evil One. God's own Son would pay with His life's blood the penalty for sin that we all deserve. All who believed on Him would be forgiven, snatched from the Enemy's clutches. Through Jesus' death and resurrection, what was lost in Eden would be restored— never fully in this life, but one day without blemish in the new Heaven and earth of God's coming Kingdom. Surely this is amazing grace.

How wondrous that the heart of our Father-God longs after the hidden hearts of His children. He continues to seek us out to offer us forgiveness through His Son so we can be restored to relationship with Him. And when our hearts are reunited with His, we as men and women can also enjoy renewed relationships with one another as well. That is the hope of the gospel. The question is how we can appropriate the gospel in our hearts and in our relationships.

I had a man tell me once that if every man would do what God calls him to do as a father, husband, or friend, there would be no unhappy women, no divorces, no broken families. Of course, I have only to look into my own soul to recognize the error of that man's judgment. Where is it written that women are less sinful than men? We women often act as though that's true; one woman said she used to approach her husband's faults with the attitude that women only commit misdemeanors, while men always commit felonies. But God isn't fooled. We women no less than men need a Savior, because we no less than men have our hearts bent on living solely for ourselves.

To understand our need for the good news of Christ's atoning death in our stead, we must acknowledge that we have sinned, recognizing that our sin has separated us from God. However, it's also important that we discern what it is in us that keeps us from experiencing the closeness with our Father for which we long and for which we were designed.

OUR NEED FOR GOSPEL
Generally, when we think of being separated from God because of our sin, what comes to mind are the things we have done or left undone, the words we have spoken or left

unsaid, the thoughts we have entertained or tried not to think. To be sure, examining our thoughts, words, and deeds is appropriate in acknowledging our sinfulness before God. But it hardly goes deep enough.

Our inferior performance is not where we as God's children are fundamentally cut off from our heavenly Father. If wrong words and deeds were the essence of our sinfulness, then the Pharisees, with their commitment to clean living and their concerted efforts to keep all the religious rules, would have received Jesus' highest commendation instead of His most impassioned denunciation. They worked harder than anyone else to look good and do everything perfectly right. But they were not connected to the Father, nor to His Son.

I believe we as women risk falling into a similar trap. We have exhausted ourselves trying to please God with our *doing* instead of just *being*, sitting quietly in His presence and enjoying His delight in us. Was not this the energy behind Jesus' friend Martha being "distracted by all the preparations that had to be made" for the dinner party planned for Jesus and His disciples (Luke 10:40)? Too busy to enjoy the One she hoped to bless, Martha ended up not only angry that her sister Mary wasn't helping her, but resentful that Jesus Himself didn't appreciate her efforts nor endorse her agenda.

"Lord, don't you care that my sister has left me to do the work by myself?" Martha accused the perfect Lover of her soul. "Tell her to help me!" she angrily commanded the Lord of the universe (10:40).

But Jesus, reflecting the heart of His heavenly Father, would not be bullied by her self-righteous indignation nor consider Himself obligated by her demands. Speaking her name twice (an indication that she was dear to Him), Jesus gently but pointedly addressed the heart issue of her attempts to earn His love by her busy doing. "'Martha, Martha,' the Lord answered, 'you are worried and upset about many things, but only one thing is needed. Mary has chosen what is better, and it will not be taken away from her'" (10:41-42).

And all perfectionists since then must look at their own hearts and ask, *Are we not worried and upset about many things—even good things—by which we think to please the God we long to serve? And does He not ask for one thing only—our hearts' devotion and adoration of Him, lived out not in our doing for Him but in our receiving from Him?*

This is a heart issue, and to find out where our separation from God cuts most deeply, we must consider Jesus' words to the Pharisees recorded in the Matthew 12. They had just explained away Jesus' healing of a demon-possessed man by saying His power came from Beelzebub, the prince of demons, not from God (12:24). Jesus' response to their blasphemy went well beneath the surface of what was going on with these self-righteously wicked men: "You brood of vipers," He said, "how can you who are evil say anything good? For out of the overflow of the heart the mouth speaks" (12:34). It was not just what the Pharisees said that was sinful; Jesus looked at their *hearts,* and the set of those hearts in opposition to Him is what He named as the core of their depravity. His severe words constituted God's merciful invitation for them to repent of what was stubbornly wrong in their hearts, so they could turn to Him for grace.

We are all invited to do likewise, to look within and see that our hearts' bent away from believing that God is good and away from trusting in His love revealed in His Son, Jesus—this bentness is the fundamental sin that separates us from Him. Certainly we think and say and do wicked things, but those things flow out of our fearful and compromised hearts. We have broken relationship with the perfect Relater, hesitating to give Him our hearts, doubting His love because we can't control it. We withhold ourselves from our truest Lover, the One Adam and Eve first adored, the One we, too, are created to worship above any other. And when He sees our doubting, fearful hearts, His own Father-heart is both angered by our foolish disbelief and broken with sorrowful longing.

We, no less than the Pharisees, must consider the heart-source of our words and actions. Surely, at times, we have done damage to men. Surely we have harmed our own souls by refusing to be responders. But our deepest sin is our unwillingness to respond with gladness to the pursuing heart of God because we don't believe He loves us as much as we need to be loved. We have done wickedly, not just in performing bad deeds, but in turning our affection to the pursuit of whatever we think will be more advantageous to our lives than God could be. Our greatest sin is our greatest loss: We have embraced false gods and severed our relationship with the One who alone is our source of life—not just our daily breath, but our daily heart's joy. We've left the perfect Lover of our souls, and our cheating hearts have made fools of us all.

FAITHLESS HEARTS

Consider our idolatrous infidelity regarding God. Designed to long for and enjoy life through our connection with the loving heart of God, we instead find ourselves terrified to need a God we cannot control. He is not only invisible, but utterly ungovernable. His love for us, though steady as His Name, cannot be commanded, only reciprocated; cannot be earned, only received. We find it intolerable to live at the mercy of grace, invited into the mystery of a divine relationship in which the mastery of religious protocol proves irrelevant to God's passion for our hearts. Our heavenly Lover's sovereign unmanageability runs contrary to every strategy by which we normally sustain our lives.

And so we go in search of protection and provision from gods we can see, gods we can direct, gods whose favor we can buy. We are like the Israelites of old, who abandoned the God who brought them out of Egypt and offered their sacrifices to Baals they could manipulate into sending the weather they needed for their crops. They erected Asherah poles and acted out with "sacred" prostitutes the fertility rites they thought would provoke the goddess to make their flocks and fields fruitful. These were gods and goddesses they could *touch;* these were things they could *do.* How much more manageable than a God who thundered from a smoking mountaintop but refused to be bullied or bought.

Our culture is for the most part post-pagan. Science has replaced Baal; genetic engineering has taken the place of Asherah. But we, the twentieth-century enlightened, are no less idolatrous. We don't keep statues in our living rooms, but we all cherish unseen icons in our hearts.

Everyone's idolatry is unique, of course, because each human heart is unique in its history of pain and style of rebellion against God. But men and women seem to pursue different kinds of idols. It is a generalization with multiple exceptions, but men seem more typically to chase after the god of personal competence. They look for a code to live by and strive for mastery so they will feel adequate to manage their world. *What can I do well, and how can I use that to make my life work?* Even in their relationships, men look for rules to follow and the right words to say. A friend told me not long ago that her husband ended an argument between them with these angry words: "Just tell me what to say that will make you happy, and I'll say it!" It did not warm her heart.

Women, on the other hand, seem more bent on worshiping the idol of relationships. *How can I connect with the people in my life in such a way as to feel loved and esteemed?* We develop our strategies for making our relationships work, because we think connectedness with people will unlock the door to our deepest happiness.

Of course it is true that women also pursue personal competence, and men are certainly concerned with relationships. But there seems to be a difference of emphasis that runs largely along gender lines—men seeking affirmation for their adequacy and women passionate to be cherished. Both inevitably look to idols instead of to God for what they think will bring them life.

WOMEN'S IDOLATRY OF MEN
Our passion to be cherished as women often leads us to worship men. Whether we are married or not, many of us put

men at the center of our hearts and lives, believing (perhaps unconsciously) that our existence is meaningless without a man to affirm our value.

If we're unmarried, for example, we may think that finding a man to love and care for us will assuage our loneliness and fill up our emptiness. As a young college graduate, I moved to a large urban community, in part because I thought it would improve my chances of finding a man who would marry me. In many ways I lived my life "on hold" until I found that man. Too often we as single women become seekers of and even pursuers after men in order to make ourselves feel lovable. We idolize marriage instead of the One who thought it up, expecting that a husband who loves us will prove both God's love for us and our own worthiness to be loved.

But singles aren't the only women who worship men. We have all known married women whose mentality suggests, "My husband is my god, and I am his unworthy slave." Such women obviously do not trust God with their lives, or they would be less afraid to rock the marital boat by being real persons who know and live out of their intrinsic value to God and their sense of inner beauty. Leanne Payne said, "It's so easy for women not to expect anything from God and instead to want everything from their husbands." And how easy it is for those women, then, to blame their husbands' shortcomings for their own feminine failure to love God and to bless others with their kindness. Cynthia Heald observed, "When God sits down with me, He's not going to say, 'Let's talk about Jack.' So I won't be able to say, 'Well, if he had been a better Christian, I would have walked more closely with You.' That's why it's so important for my heart and my eyes to be on Jesus." God wants our undivided loyalty, and a wife's idolatry of her husband is neither a blessing to him nor acceptable to a jealous God who will brook no rivals.

And what about the unhappily married woman who focuses her life's energy not on pleasing God and serving others but on changing her husband into the man she thinks will make her happy? She clings to the illusion that an improved husband or a different man or perhaps the freedom of singleness will somehow diminish her pain and bring her the happiness she feels she deserves. This is often the energy behind our strategies to control or change men: We are trying to shore up the idols we have made, trying to make men into "good gods" we can manipulate to make our lives smooth and problem-free.

Even happily married women sometimes experience a vague emptiness in their lives, and they entertain the occasional notion that maybe something "more" from their relationships with men will dissipate the discontent. In fact, the woman married to a good man is perhaps the most puzzled of all in her idolatry, because she finds herself dissatisfied when she knows she should be grateful. What she often fails to recognize is that even good men make terrible gods.

Strangely enough, at the opposite end of the spectrum, the worship of the male can sometimes be seen in women who disdain men, yet become like men themselves in the ways they move into their world. We can become caught up in our envy of men, worshiping, if not the men themselves, then at least their positions of masculine power and their opportunities in the world. Moreover, if imitation is the highest form of praise, even some women who speak negatively about men but stride through their lives in manly ways are giving double messages regarding what they really think of the opposite sex.

Men are very important to our lives as women, and God's intention was good when He designed us male and female and brought us together. Men play a significant role in our lives, helping to shape who we are and how we see ourselves, bringing us rich satisfaction when they come to us with their hearts. But they are not God and can never be God. When we make them our gods, we frustrate them with our impossible expectations and prostitute our hearts from our first love.

Unfortunately, because we can't always discern how to love men without worshiping them, we often move in our relationships with them neither recognizing nor addressing our often unconscious belief that they are deities who have the power to bring life or destruction to our souls.

OTHER FEMININE IDOLATRIES

On the other hand, men being mere mortals, we women find ourselves time and again faced with their inability or unwillingness to be the gods we demand they be to make us feel loved. And when our relationships with men disappoint us, we sometimes turn to other relationships to satisfy our hunger to feel valued. Some of us may, for example, invest all our hope and energy in our children, seeking solace in their love for us. But our mother-love can easily become a weapon by which we hold our children hostage to make ourselves feel loved and accepted. And in using them to meet our needs, we neglect our God-ordained responsibility to parent them by meeting *their* needs.

Perhaps we turn to our female friendships to give meaning to our lives. Women, after all, will listen to our hearts in ways men often will not. But turning to women who love and value our hearts can also be a set-up for idolatry. A friendship we think we cannot live without can become our god. A friend once commented, "I suppose there isn't a woman alive, married or single, who hasn't at one time or another been disappointed in her relationships with men. But for us to abandon men and turn our whole focus to relationships with other women is not a viable option if we are Christians. Going to God must be our first priority, then longing for relationships with good men, even while we enjoy our female friendships."

Hard words but wise. We certainly need female friends in our lives, but friends who will point us to God and encourage us to go on desiring relationships with men. My friends love me, and I intentionally bring my soul to them so they can speak into my life. But they are the best kind of friends, because they always direct my heart back to my husband, Bill, even when I'm disappointed in him.

I do the same with them. I encourage my married friends to find appropriate ways to ask their husbands for the love they long to receive. And I remind my single friends to pray that God will give them men in their lives who will act as a godly covering for them—fathers or brothers or married couples who will pray for them and offer their perspective and protection for their lives. My friends and I recognize that if we were to become the only emotional support for one another, it would do damage to our feminine hearts, which are designed to stay responsive to masculine hearts. Maintaining the balance of enjoying our female friendships while keeping our hearts open to men is often difficult. We must ask our heavenly Father for a sustained softness toward good men and for purity in all of our friendships.

Of course, we women have made idols out of more than just our relationships. We have worshiped whatever we think will satisfy our souls, whether home or children, job or financial security, success or ministry—even our pursuit of a godly Christian life. Ultimately, the infidelity against God embryonic in all other idolatries is worship of ourselves, of our own personal comfort, of our right to run our lives as we think best without needing God. Rather than struggle to find our comfort in God, we look to our own resources to sustain our lives. Seduced from trusting His heart, we find ourselves separated from *real* life with Him. And this unwarranted devotion to self-sufficiency is the deepest insult of all to the gracious heart of God, who longs to have us enter His rest.

It is this, our idolatry, that has put us in need of the gospel. Jesus had to die in order to pay the price for every man's worship of his own competence. The Cross is necessary to pay for every woman's obsession with her relationships in preference to finding life in the Father's love. That doesn't mean men should be incompetent nor that women should suppress their longing for relational connectedness. It just means that neither mastery nor human beings can be God. As one woman told me, "The bottom line is that God is the only One who can really meet our needs, and we must go back to Him with our hearts." All other idols, all our false gods, must be destroyed. We need a Savior who will deliver us from our sin.

FORSWEARING OUR IDOLS

Because God is jealously relentless for our hearts' single devotion, He will not leave our infidelity unchallenged. Rest in Him requires that we renounce our spiritual infidelities. We cannot have it both ways. We cannot worship ourselves or our competence or our relationships or our *anything* and still find the rest we long to receive in the arms of our Father. We have to make a choice.

Isaiah encourages us as God's people to abandon our idolatry and turn to Him in repentance, promising that then we will taste His grace. "How gracious he will be when you cry for help! As soon as he hears, he will answer you" (Isaiah 30:19). And what God will do when we cry out, the answer He will give when He hears our repentant pleas for help—this is the most wondrous saving of all: He Himself will come. The God of the universe will Himself be seen and heard by us in familiar ways our idols can never even approximate. "Although the Lord gives you the bread of adversity and the water of affliction," Isaiah promises on God's behalf, "your teachers will be hidden no more; with your own eyes you will see them. Whether you turn to the right or to the left, your ears will hear a voice behind you, saying, 'This is the way; walk in it'" (30:20-21). Imagine! The infinite God so immanently present that, even in our adversity, we can hear Him whispering in our ears, making the Real God real to our hearts.

And when Reality has broken in, how can we go back to the unreal? No idol promising the illusion of control and safety can compare to the intimate Whisperer in our ears whose presence is comfort when all is out of control, whose love is all the safety we need. Isaiah predicts what will become of our idols when we embrace the Real: "Then you will defile your idols overlaid with silver and your images covered with gold; you will throw them away like a menstrual cloth and say to them, 'Away with you!'" (30:22).

What a scandalous image! When we repent and turn to our only true Lover, our false gods will seem repulsive to us, and we will not hesitate to cast them away time and again in preference to the Reality of God's coming.

GOD'S DESIGN REINSTATED

But the good news doesn't end with the proclamation that when our hearts are captivated by our Savior's love, we will repent of our spiritual adultery, detest all other heart affections, and become fit candidates for Heaven. Not content to merely save us from eternal death, the God of glory has a larger purpose: the restoration of His original design for relationships that will reflect His own ineffable unity-in-diversity type of relating within the Trinity.

First, of course, He draws us as His female image-bearers back into intimacy with Himself. When He whispers in our ears through the inner voice of His Holy Spirit, our feminine hearts leap at the voice of the One we adore. We will recognize the voice as His if we will take the time to listen, if we will be Mary at His feet instead of Martha in the kitchen. Our deepest joy is found when we are desperate for Him, when we recognize we cannot go on if He does not come to us. And often our recognition of our desire for Him comes as we give words to others regarding what He has done for us and Who He is to us.

Christian poet Luci Shaw and I were sharing a cup of coffee in the sunshine flooding her California kitchen when she asked, "Do you know what the essence of good friendship is to me?" Answering her own question, she then said, "God talk and book talk."

I loved the comment. I believe God talk (and often book talk, too) is important to Christian women. We have a passionate desire both to experience and to put words to our personal intimacy with God. God portrays Himself in Scripture as the pursuing Lover of our souls, and we yearn to receive His love. Luci spoke to this, too, saying, "I think God wants us to come to Him in the full vigor of our personality and to abandon ourselves to Him as vessels for His use." Longing to abandon our hearts to His love is rich evidence of our intrinsically responsive nature as women.

Single women, especially, are invited to experience God as the Lover of their hearts. My good friend, Mary Ann Ulmer, told me that when she moved to a new city where she had not yet developed close relationships, she found rich comfort in God's words to her heart, "I will be your friend." Pamela Reeve described her walk with God in these words: "As a single woman I have gone directly to the Lord as the One to encourage and protect me, and to fight my battles for me, and I have found Him tremendously enabling. The most important thing to me in the entire universe is His love." Rich words from a woman rich in faith and in the intimate knowledge of her Lord!

RENEWED DESIRE FOR GOOD MEN
But our reawakened hunger for God is not the only consequence of our redemption. As we listen and respond to the holy Wooer of our hearts, we are changed so that our relationships can be restored on many different levels. We can learn to reveal God's own commitment to the good of others, even those we formerly feared and thus hated—people who are not like us, people whom we do not understand or with whom we disagree, even people who have done us harm.

Others may refuse our kindness, and the restoration process may be blocked or tediously slow, but God is nonetheless pleased with our desire as women to know healing in our relationships. Because He repeatedly describes Himself in relational images, the changes He brings about in our hearts through His presence in us will always bring about change in our feminine connections—as daughters, as sisters, as wives, as mothers, as friends, as parishioners, as workers.

But it is in our restored relationships with men that God's original design for us as women is most intimately reinstated. In spite of the Fall, God's blueprint for His female image-bearers is that they desire what men are designed to bring to them—their hearts, their strength, and their kindness. We women have what one woman described as "an insatiable appetite in our hearts to be intimately connected to a man." We desire it because God made us to desire it. Someone has described the mystery of relationship in these words: "When a man and a woman connect, the world becomes more round."

But it won't always be easy. The Fall has thrown a cog into the machinery of male-female relationships. "It takes a lot of energy to make the differences between us as men and women work *for* instead of *against* our relating," declared Jane Berry. "Sometimes it's such a pain in the neck, we'd just as soon go our own way and leave it alone. But the distinction is really a jewel, and we don't always realize how wonderful it is."

Valerie Bell, a musician, author, and conference speaker, summed it up best when she said "We must come to the place where we can say, 'This man is the opposite of me and we drive each other crazy. But it is God's plan, and it is right.'"

Our coming together as men and women has always been God's plan, and it has always been right. "Men and women are both created in God's image," a friend reminded me recently, "and when the two together use that as the basis of their relationship, the fruit of their oneness brings joy to God's heart." Indeed. God still declares His relational design "very good."

Thus, we reflect not only our *created* nature, but also our *redeemed* nature when we desire the movement of good men toward us. More than that, our desire for good men to come to us is a mirror image of our desire for God to come to us. God won't force us to respond to Him, but He is passionately relentless to win us to Himself. And our longing to receive His love is reflected in our longing to receive that kind of love from good men, too.

It is not shameful for us to admit we need and desire

men, but it is *good* men we desire, men who have a heart for God. "The thing I want most from men, whether my husband or any other man, is for them to pursue God," said Barbara Fletcher. "It sounds so simplistic, but with all my heart I believe when that's happening, the other things will fall into place."

Another woman summed up our feminine hunger for good men in these words: "I'm so drawn by men who have a passion for God, who have taken the time to find out who God is and have done the hard work of saying, 'I'll stay here until you come, Lord. I'm not leaving until you bless me.' A man who has waited for God is a man who will pursue a woman and do the hard work of capturing her heart. It is such a reflection of the immutability of God, who never wavers in His love toward us."

There is something about a man's passion for God that deeply blesses us as women. Perhaps it is because we know that men who pursue the heart of God will also move toward our own hearts on God's behalf and in His way and with His tender energy. "What attracted me to my husband was his passion for the Lord," said Holly Phillips, whose husband, Randy, is president of Promise Keepers. "If he weren't living for Jesus, I wouldn't have any security."

My friend, Penny Freeman, said it this way: "When I look down from my church balcony and see men worship, it moves me in a very deep way. I think it has to do with safety. When I see men let themselves really enjoy God, I know I'm safe, and I want to weep with joy."

Our redeemed feminine hearts respond to these women's words with yearning. We long for men who, because of their relationship with God, can reflect to us the kind steadiness of God's love for us. That is our heart's deep desire—not just relationship with *any* man, but with a good man who loves God more than he loves us, yet who will not hesitate to come to our hearts because God has come to his.

WHEN GOOD MEN DON'T COME

Sadly, some women have not tasted relationships like these very often—perhaps not at all. They may not even want to desire that kind of love because they don't believe they will ever experience it. Perhaps they've found themselves in a marriage that is deeply disappointing, even abusive, and they struggle to merely survive each day. For such women, words about desiring good men may prompt either cynical laughter or heart-piercing pain. I have talked with countless such women and have grappled with similar issues in my own life.

Where is the hope of the gospel for women who don't have good men and who see no possibility of ever being loved by a man with gentle strength? Surely each relationship is unique and no simple answers exist. But some women may need to seek professional help in breaking out of destructive patterns of relating so that the gospel can penetrate their hearts in new ways. Abusive relationships bless neither the abused nor the abuser.

Other women may need to take a closer look at what they are doing with their relational disappointment. If they have become contemptuous about being loved, they can examine why they have chosen cynicism over sadness. If they have shut down their longing, they can choose whether to stay dead. If they are grieving their loss and are in great pain, they can find comfort in inviting the God who groaned in Gethsemane to walk their path with them.

But all of us, whether connected to good men or not, can affirm the design: We all in our deepest hearts want to be God's women, in love with Him and open to the hearts of good men, even though our own wounded hearts often get in the way of our desires. My friend Jody Engel, a Christian counselor living in Anderson, Indiana, put these words to our dilemma: "The energy many of us spend on rage is about the death of hope that we can live as women loved by men. We don't believe there are any good men, nor is there a good God, so we stop longing for either and learn to depend on ourselves.

"But when I learned what God created men to do and what gifts He intended them to bring," Jody affirmed, "I saw something wonderful about the heart of a man. Then my longing for connectedness with a good man was stirred, and I knew I wanted to respond as a woman to that kind of man. As men learn how to move kindly toward our hearts, they will disrupt by their goodness those of us who are weary and disillusioned so that we can receive the good news of the gospel of God's love for us."

We always need the gospel. To find hope for our relationships with men, we must hear again that the long-promised Christ has crushed the head of the Evil One. By Jesus' death and resurrection God has thwarted the Enemy's wicked agenda and has desecrated his wretched shrines. Moreover, God's design for His children's relationships has not been obliterated. Redeemed men can and do know themselves competent in work and in their kind movement toward the hearts of women. And our feminine longing for intimacy—the very thing that draws us to God's heart—can yet respond to the hearts of good men. What God created He also can redeem, snatching our affections away from our idols, channeling our desire to Himself and then, by His Spirit, toward one another.

This is the glory of God and our sure hope!

———

Believing it is God's kindness that draws us
to repentance for the sake of the gospel, may we seek
His wisdom to recognize our hearts' idolatries,
His gift of humility to confess them, and the
resoluteness of His Spirit to relinquish them for His
glory and our truest comfort.

———

QUESTIONS FOR REFLECTION AND DISCUSSION

God is most surely the seeker after our compromised and faithless hearts toward Him. But His seeking is both welcome and disquieting to us. When He comes to us with His grace, He also comes with His flintlike anger to spark our own hatred toward the idolatry that separates our hearts from His. Every heart, therefore, must face these questions: Do you believe you are separated from God by your sin and are unable to save yourself? Do you believe Jesus of Nazareth died for your sin, taking your place on the cross to bear the penalty of that sin? If you have not done so before, are you willing to ask Him now to be your Savior and Lord, inviting Him to take up residence in your heart? No other questions are more important to answer.

But we are also invited to continue to examine our hearts' true devotion, so ponder and discuss these questions as well.

1. How are you expecting (perhaps demanding) that God will respond to your most diligent efforts to earn His love by obeying the Bible's commands?
2. What experiences have you had in which, out of the overflow of your disappointed heart, your mouth has spoken unkind or vindictive words?
3. Did that unintended exposure of your heart move you to repentance or to excuses and self-vindication?
4. What evidence, if any, is there in your life that you have made men or men's power an idol?
5. How has your deification of men harmed or blessed them?
6. How might your relationships with women keep you from embracing your desire for good men and a good God?
7. In what ways have you experienced God breaking into your life with the startling reality of His presence?
8. How have you responded to His coming?

9. Are there idols that still keep you from experiencing His reality?
10. Why is it hard for you to rest in God's love?

PART TWO

Moving Toward Integrity

CHAPTER FOUR

OUR ENTRANCE INTO REALITY: EMBRACING AUTHENTICITY

*God's promise is that I can be honest with Him
and He will still love me.*
DALE HANSON BOURKE

"*I* don't think we know what we really believe about God until we experience some crisis, which is the test and the definer of our theology," said Valerie Bell, as we shared our hearts over tea in her living room in Wheaton, Illinois. "At twenty-six I had my first real crisis—my father getting ill with encephalitis that totally burned out his brain. The devastation of losing my father mentally left me with a lot of anger at God. I had lived thinking if I was good, God would be the spiritual snowplow smoothing out the path in front of me, and now I felt He hadn't kept His side of the bargain.

"I remember a terrible scene at the nursing home," she continued. "My father was in a straitjacket and I could hear him screaming from the parking lot. I just got into my car, went about two blocks, pulled my car over, and cried out to God: 'This is a scam! My father served You all his life and he never got a retirement! I don't believe in You anymore!' I was a pastor's wife without any faith. Talk about uncomfortable!

"Yet I was desperate for some indication that God

existed, and sometime later God did give me a touch—He intervened in a special way with our baby, who had been born with some health problems. It wasn't the prayer I had been praying, but something out of the ordinary happened in my life, and I decided to take the risk and see if my belief in God could be renewed.

"Our prayers don't always get answered in the way we expect or would like," Valerie concluded, "but that doesn't mean God is uncaring or distant. He leads us and loves us right through the personal hells we live through."

It is a mark of Valerie's integrity that she did not pretend about how she felt when God put His finger on a relationship important to her, taking things out of her control. He did not hurry her back to faith, but came to her in the midst of her doubt to touch her with His presence and to give her hope. How like a good father He is!

HOPE AMIDST FALLENNESS
Why would I include a story about a woman's profound bereavement in a book about encouragement? "Where is the encouragement in *that?*" someone may ask.

For countless women who have struggled with God regarding their memories of loss or abandonment by men (even if unintentional), it is a question begging for an answer. If God is calling His sons to become ambassadors of the gospel of reconciliation, He is just as surely calling His daughters to cooperate with what He is doing in His world. If we find ourselves resisting God's movement, it may be because we distrust His intentions toward us. Some early experience of disruption may have unconsciously affected what we think of God. As Valerie said, what we most deeply believe about God is often tested and defined in the context of the crises God allows into our lives.

We want to believe God is good. We want to believe there are reasons for our tragedies, reasons that will help us understand who God is and give us hope for our future. But some of us wonder if anything can redeem the losses of our past.

Even as we look for ways to alleviate our present pain, we may question what kind of future we can legitimately hope for in a broken world. These are issues Scripture does not hesitate to address, though what God has to say may not be at all what we expect.

We must not, of course, lose our balance along the way. Life does not consist merely in moving from crisis to crisis so we can know God better. Part of the wondrous mystery of relationships is that they are emotionally multifaceted. We experience intimacy with people and with God in our glad moments as well as in our sorrow and anger. When we fall in love or get a raise or hold a baby or welcome home a wayward child, our hearts leap within us and we rejoice with those we love, turning grateful eyes to meet the smile in God's countenance. The tapestry of our life's relationships, human and divine, is woven together through a variety of interactions experienced in a diversity of circumstances.

But I've found that when life is going smoothly, my times of enjoying people and connecting with God inevitably leave me somewhat pensive, because they do not last. I want to package my pleasure and save it for later, but I have lived long enough to know that my best days—and even my sweetest tastes of intimacy with God—can be neither prolonged nor duplicated. Does God come to us in our moments of joy? Certainly. But we err if we conclude that when our lives are not going smoothly, God is displeased with us, impatient that we learn how to better cooperate with Him so He can give us the happiness we've come to expect as His promise for this life.

It is easy to misunderstand God's promises. Mary Kassian tells this story of her childhood disappointment when she had expectations of God that were not correct: "I vividly remember as a little girl praying I would win a raffle for a particular stuffed animal I'd fallen in love with, and it didn't happen. I was crushed, and it threw my faith for a loop—*God, what are You doing?* I wanted to know. I see the same pattern in my adult life: I have a stuffed-animal picture of what I want, and when it doesn't materialize, I wonder what God is doing.

"But," Mary explained, "God never promises to give us everything we ask for. What He promises is to care for us and change who we are as we open our hearts and submit to Him, enabling us to deal with whatever comes our way because we are intact. *That* is what He promises to us."

We must never forget that fullness of joy cannot be ours until we get Home. The danger of false expectations is that we may feel compelled to prove God's goodness by showing how happy we are, rather than showcasing His goodness by trusting Him even when we are unhappy at having to live in a world broken by sin. We are right to pursue a full-orbed relationship with God, engaging with Him not just when there is reason to rejoice, but coming honestly to Him when our circumstances and emotions are in disarray as well.

This is precisely the pattern we see in God's relationship with His people throughout Scripture. He came to Sarah in the futility of her barrenness, and to her daughter-in-law, Rebekah, in the same kind of circumstance. Jacob didn't wrestle with God until his brother was heading toward him with four hundred armed men. Joseph became desperate for God in prison, Moses in the desert, Hannah in her anguish, Ruth in her widowhood, David in the wilderness, Elijah in his flight from Jezebel, Paul in his blindness. Surely those men and women of God knew His blessing in times of peace and comfort, but the people God uses mightily are those who also know Him in the direst of circumstances. We stand in good company when we enter the reality of our lives and learn how to suffer well. Jesus Himself "learned obedience from what he suffered" (Hebrews 5:8), and we are invited to "follow in his steps" (1 Peter 2:21) by suffering according to God's design.

We learn to suffer well whenever we allow what God sends into our lives to propel us toward taking a closer look at Him and at our hearts. This is a book about encouragement and hope. But genuine hope is a hope hard won, a hope not in a revised childhood nor changed circumstances nor improved relationships, but in a God who died for us and promised His presence with us in *any* circumstance, no matter what. This God invites us to face whatever anger or sorrow there might be in us regarding the losses we have experienced, particularly in our relationships with Him and with men.

If we as God's daughters have lost hope, we cannot experience its revival without first moving into reality, especially the painful truth that we bear the consequences of living in a fallen world. It is a reality we generally find difficult but necessary to face if we are to receive for ourselves and offer to others the splendid hope of the gospel. It is always hopeful when God disrupts us, for it is His kind grace that calls us to answer with our own life choices His penetrating question: "What do you love more than Me?"

GOD'S STRATEGY OF GRACE
How do we enter the reality that will usher us into hope? Perhaps a more basic question is, Are we willing to face the disappointment and anger we may find in our hearts as we enter that reality? Sometimes we do not know the answer until we find ourselves in a situation we cannot control. "I have learned it's when I'm up against the wall that I come to trust God at deeper levels," said Kathy Peel, Christian author and lecturer. "Our sinful human condition is often very painful, and if I want to know God better, I have to face my pain, looking to God for His help and trying to grasp the truth that He is in it and He is working."

We must not forget God's passion: He is relentless to destroy our false gods, jealous for His Name and for our hearts' single devotion. Our sin has its own painful consequences, and God may allow those consequences to fall as His invitation to repent and turn to Him for grace.

But sometimes our pain is not the direct result of our own sin, but of the larger reality of living in a world that groans under the weight of Satan's tyranny. In this, too, God invites us to examine our devotion to Him. In His kindness He allows disruption into our lives to dismantle our emotional and spiritual complacency for the sake of confronting us again and again with the ugliness of sin and the wonder of His gospel. Thus our calamities become a work of God's grace as we seek His higher purpose in them.

Those of us who want to face our sorrow with integrity must be willing to let God move us in directions we may not want to go. He is our guide on this journey, and He has much to teach and offer if we are willing to relinquish our commitment to stay out of pain.

Pain is usually considered our enemy, the disrupter and destroyer of our lives. When we think back to events that caused us pain, either physically or emotionally, it's natural not to want to feel that way again.

But our dogged commitment not to enter the painfulness of our disappointments is both futile and destructive. We damage ourselves if we refuse to acknowledge the disappointment and anger our hearts feel at the intrusion of loss—a death, abandonment by someone we love, a wayward child, the recurring memory of past abuse, or some other unsettling event. We then must choose whether or not we will face the loss and bring our broken hearts to God.

Our pain repeatedly raises questions about our relationship with God. The coming of any calamity to our lives is an invitation to look at how we feel about God—a look we might never take otherwise. Dale Hanson Bourke spoke candidly of the tragedy God sent into her life that revealed God's willingness to hear her anger when her heart was broken. "My relationship with God has really changed in the last seven or eight years," Dale said. "I went through an experience I didn't have answers for: I lost a baby. And I remember saying to God, 'I'm really angry at You! You're not the God I thought You were—so who are You?'

"Until I got to that level, I couldn't have an honest relationship with God," Dale went on. "I had struggled with doubts before and had tried to suppress them. But now I don't experience doubts at that same level, because I don't pretend anymore that God doesn't know what my true feelings are.

"Yet I feel secure in God's love," she affirmed. "I know He wants the best for me, even when I have to face great pain. He is trying to make me into His image, and sometimes it hurts a lot to move me in that direction. But I'm sure He's going to be there and stay with me."

Surely we recoil at the evidence we see of brokenness in our world, especially in those relationships vital to us as women. Even when we try to live as God has called us to live, we have no guarantee that our good behavior will protect us from bad things happening to us. And in our hardships, God invites us to candor—to look into our hearts, to face our anger and our doubts, and to bring Him our words about how we are feeling. It is an honesty that can open us to God's presence and strengthen our faith if we will enter our sorrow and ask Him to come along with us.

FACING RELATIONAL DAMAGE

It is one thing to enter our anger and sorrow about relational losses that are no one's "fault"—a father's encephalitis or a child's death or the loss of a parent at an early age. One woman told me, "Because my mother was widowed young and I had no father to direct my energy, I responded to the whole world as a woman, and in my naiveté I made a bad marriage that did not last."

But there are relational losses we as women endure that are the result of men's choices not to love us or perhaps even to do us harm. In their masculine reflection of God's image as initiators, penetrators, and word-givers, men have sometimes been incited by the enemy to move toward women (and sometimes little girls) to *use* them instead of to *bless* them. As women image God by being responders who long to be enjoyed, this can be twisted by the Enemy so that we respond to the wrong people or in ways that do us harm. For example, Edith Schaeffer, widow of Francis

Schaeffer and an author living in Rochester, Minnesota, had these words to say about sexual abuse in the home: "You can't allow a child to be sexually abused just because the man is the head of the home. That breaks his place and he is no longer a representative of Christ to the Church. It is a terrible travesty, and it will destroy the children. They will never want to embrace Christianity. They will say, *If this is Christianity, let me out.*" When men use God's good gifts selfishly instead of unselfishly, we as women must face the damage it does to us.

Men also wound women when they make promises they do not keep. One woman, commenting on the importance of men's marital vows, said succinctly, "The promise to be there and not to escape is kind of primary." Divorce is a painful reality in the lives of countless Christians today, and though men are surely not the only ones responsible for breaking covenant with their mates, often the divorced woman faces overwhelming obstacles in recovering from the damage of that broken relationship.

A woman once spoke these candid words to me about the plight of the divorcee: "A divorced woman is perceived as a threat, even in the Church, because her presence is a reminder that everyone is susceptible and every marriage is fragile. She must be given time and support as she mourns her loss, because even if the marriage had turned sour, there were good things in it for which she will have reason to grieve.

"A divorced or rejected woman knows something intimate about the heart of God," she went on to say, "because she, like God, has loved someone who walked away from her. We in the Church must treat her with respect and great kindness, remembering that it is only by the grace of God that we are even moderately successful in any relationship." Insightful words from a woman who herself had been deeply wounded.

Evidence abounds that we share a fallen world with fallen

men, and when they hurt us, we have *feelings* about it. If we ignore those feelings we do harm to our hearts.

ASKING HARD QUESTIONS

Some women wonder why they should even address negative feelings. They'd like to forget how men may have failed or abandoned them. They think somehow it will just shame men if they dredge up old disappointments. Or they may feel they're just being judgmental.

To take it a step further, doesn't Scripture emphasize reconciliation among believers? This talk about entering our disappointment seems to go directly contrary to Paul's teaching that love 'keeps no record of wrongs' (1 Corinthians 13:5). After all, Jesus told Peter he had to forgive seventy-seven times (Matthew 18:22). How can we obey Paul's admonition to respect our husbands (Ephesians 5:33) and Peter's instruction to be submissive (1 Peter 3:1) if we face and give words to our anger and sorrow?"

I have asked these questions myself, and for years I answered them by keeping myself well managed emotionally, if somewhat sterile spiritually. I wanted my life both orderly and flawless. Avoiding my feelings enabled me to accomplish that goal—or at least it offered me the illusion of having accomplished that goal.

But was I doing what God had called me to do? I'm not at all sure He expected my life to be neat and perfect. If God's very nature is relational (three Persons so perfectly related that they are one God), then we must seek to recognize those things that either enhance or block His relationship with us as His image-bearers. What does Scripture record as being God's prerequisite for entering and sustaining relationship with His people? Was their emotional orderliness necessary?

We must remember that God came to Adam and Eve in the Garden of Eden when their shameful confusion was at its height, showing Himself to them in the midst of their strong emotions. He did not give up on Sarai when she said to Abram (most likely with an edge in her voice), "The LORD has kept me from having children. Go, sleep with my maidservant; perhaps I can build a family through her" (Genesis 16:2). God was not reluctant to speak with Hagar in the desert, even in the context of her rebellion against and flight from her mistress, Sarai (16:6-14). His wrestling with Jacob was not passive (Genesis 32), nor did He strike Job dead when he angrily demanded that God justify Himself (Job 23). Not all of David's psalms were hymns of praise; consider Psalm 69. Elijah was not chided for his depression (1 Kings 19), nor did God withdraw from Jeremiah when he cursed the day of his birth (Jeremiah 20:14). The patriarchs, the chroniclers, the prophets, and most especially the psalmists held nothing back in their dialogue with the Almighty, and God neither shamed them for it nor withheld Himself from them until they could manage to get themselves emotionally stabilized.

The theme is repeated in the New Testament. Consider Martha's complaint when Jesus allowed her sister Mary to sit at His feet. Jesus was not disappointed in Martha; He did not withdraw from her because of her honesty. Nor did He rebuke His disciples for their outspoken interactions with Him. He did not forsake Peter because of his denial, nor Thomas because of his doubt. And what of Paul's agony over his "thorn in the flesh," or the impassioned cry of the martyred saints under the altar, agonizing before God, "How long, Sovereign Lord, holy and true, until you judge the inhabitants of the earth and avenge our blood?" (Revelation 6:10)?

God's people have never been dispassionate about what they were experiencing, and God did not punish them for their emotional intensity. Rather, He invited them to face with integrity what was going on in their inner lives. He not only engaged with them, He even encouraged them to struggle with Him. He seldom gave them what they demanded, and certainly not on their timetable. But in the reality of their emotional candor, He came to them and showed them

His heart of sacrificial love. *That* is the intimacy we long for and can have with this unmanageable Lover of our souls.

ATTENDING TO RELATIONSHIPS

One way we can develop a deeper intimacy with God is to look honestly at the relationships we have in our lives—with our parents, with our spouses, with our friends, with our children. We can ask ourselves what emotions they evoke in us at any given moment, and why. We can take note of when we feel like crying and what we do when we feel like crying— or, perhaps, why we never cry. We can pay attention to what makes us afraid or what triggers our anger. We can struggle to discern whether our anger generally shames us or invigorates us or protects us or controls us. Moreover, we can examine what we do when we are angry.

These are not fundamentally questions about psychology, introspection, or even our emotions. They are questions about relationships—about how we are and *who* we are in our interactions with God and with others. They are questions about the reality and validity and nature of our relationship with God, as well as our relationships with one another.

Strange as it may seem, the way we as women experience our relationships with men profoundly reflects the way we experience our relationship with God. This is not just because God in Scripture consistently refers to Himself in masculine terms (such as Father and Son), but because our responsiveness as women toward men reflects the way God's people respond to Him—the way the Apostle Paul in Ephesians 5 says the Church responds to her Bridegroom. Our openness to receive and respond to the hearts of good men somehow matches our openness to and passion for relationship with God. Conversely, our hardness or anger toward men usually reflects our reluctance to turn to God with softened hearts. For that reason, if we will allow ourselves to grieve what disappoints us regarding men and to work toward forgiving them, we will find ourselves turning our hearts more fully toward God as well.

GOD'S FALLEN MEN

No woman, of course, has ever been fathered by or married to a perfect man. We tend to believe the grass is always greener on the other side of the relational fences that border our lives, but we are deceived in that belief. We even idealize the men we read about in the Bible, thinking they, at least, had the kind of character we wish were true of the men we know today. But we forget how very honest Scripture is about God's men.

What, for instance, did Sarai *wish* Abram had said when she suggested he sleep with Hagar (Genesis 16)? Rebekah was surely not blessed by Isaac's preference for Esau, who was not the son of the promise (Genesis 25). And I wonder what was going on between Leah and Jacob when she named her first son Reuben, saying, "It is because the LORD has seen my misery. Surely my husband will love me now" (Genesis 29:32). Why was Moses' wife the one to circumcise their son (Exodus 4)? Did Bathsheba wish David had behaved differently when he saw her on the roof of her house (2 Samuel 11)? And what about princess Tamar's loss of her father David's protection after she was raped by her step-brother Amnon (2 Samuel 13)? These men were all imperfect husbands, fathers, brothers.

To be sure there is also the biblical record of Abraham's faith (Genesis 15), Joseph's refusal to dishonor Potiphar's wife (Genesis 39), the spies' kind treatment of Rahab (Joshua 2), Boaz's goodness toward Ruth (Ruth 2–4), David's respect for Abigail (1 Samuel 25), and countless other stories of men whose redeemed hearts are showcased throughout the Old and New Testaments. All of these were God's men, yet all of them failed to consistently be what they should have been in their relationships, especially with women. Why did God show us their weaknesses as well as their strengths?

Perhaps it comes down to God revealing His glory, the glory of His grace. He has always been concerned more for our hearts than for our polished behavior, and He reminds us of that by giving us graphic stories about real-life, sinful men and women in the Bible. He does not pretend they were better than they really were. Instead He showed us their human frailty so that He could showcase His grace toward an undeserving people. As Moses reminded the Israelites, poised to enter the promised land to take it from the Canaanites, "It is not because of your righteousness or your integrity that you are going in to take possession of their land; but on account of the wickedness of these nations, the LORD your God will drive them out before you, to accomplish what he swore to your fathers, to Abraham, Isaac and Jacob. Understand, then, that it is not because of your righteousness that the LORD your God is giving you this good land to possess, for you are a stiff-necked people" (Deuteronomy 9:5-6).

What was God's point? He knew He was dealing with a people whose necks were stiff with pride and with a resistance to His embrace, a newly liberated people more used to the cruelty of a taskmaster than to the kindness of a heavenly Father. God wanted to remind this willful people about grace—His grace to Abraham and passed down to them by faith. He still reminds us today of that same grace extended to us.

We must face the deeper question about our own hearts: Do we believe we're loved by God because we're good, or are we loved by God because *He* is good? If we think we're loved because we're good, we will live under law, guilt, pressure, and under siege—held hostage by our fear of failure. We will also do the same to others, requiring their conformity to our standards before we will move toward them to bless their lives. If, on the other hand, we believe we're loved because *God* is good (though we are not), then we will live under grace, under His covering, released from fear. We will be able to love others with integrity and gratitude because of the overflow of God's love in us.

Grace is essential for all of us, and it will have implications for how honestly we dare to face the fallenness of others. None of God's people is perfect, only forgiven. Scripture is careful to point out that God's men have never been perfect—not Abraham nor Jacob nor Joseph nor Moses nor David nor *any* of them except God's Son, Jesus.

That is reality-based living—recognizing that neither we nor the men we live and work with are perfect. All of us have been harmed in some way by some of our past relationships, and we do harm in our present relationships because of that damage and because of our sinful nature. Can we as women acknowledge that reality and stop demanding that men never let us down? We must not pretend about how deeply disappointed we sometimes are, but we must also remember that God calls us to learn how to love fallen men, even as we face what is real about our hearts toward them.

FACING WHAT IS REAL

If my background is any indication of the common experience of women, it is safe to suppose we women are not always in touch with our disappointment regarding men. We tend to deny or minimize our disillusionment, not only because of the pain and disruption it would cause, but also because of our reluctance to admit how helpless we would feel if we faced the truth. Yet if we will dismantle our denial strategies, we can examine what is deeply hidden in our hearts toward men and toward God.

There is, of course, no set formula for entering the reality of "what is" instead of staying in the "I wish" of our relationships. Each woman's journey is uniquely hers and no two are alike. But I can tell you how God invited me to enter my brokenness until I became desperate for His love. It was not an easy passage.

I have lived with a man who did much harm to himself and to me because of his wounded past and his addiction to alcohol. I have also lived with a man whose heart is turned toward God and who loves me wonderfully well. They are not two men but one—my husband, Bill.

Because of my own wounded past, I spent the first fifteen years of my marriage to Bill coping with his increasing alcohol addiction by trying to stay in charge. I was sweetly manipulative, verbally relentless, and spiritually condescending. I tried to manage his life, acting more like his mother than his wife, discreetly trying to say the Holy Spirit's words I thought Bill would never hear by himself. Struggling to be a godly, submissive wife, I prayed fervently that God would change Bill into the man I thought he could and ought to be, a man I could deeply respect.

In the fifteenth year of our life together, afraid that the pattern of alcohol abuse was repeating itself in our son's life, I began the excruciating process of facing what was in my own heart that kept me from respecting Bill enough to tell him honestly of my fear and frustration about his drinking. It was not a pleasant time. Bill was furious at my changing and enraged at the people to whom I turned for support and guidance. Along my journey out of denial and into treating him like a man, I had to face the damage he and I had done to each other over the years in our wrong handling of his addictive drinking.

More than that, as I entered my terror and anger at the harm Bill's alcoholism was doing, I began also to experience a conscious recollection of the damage other men had done to me over the years. Once I opened the door to my feelings about Bill, I realized there were other things in my life, events in my past I *ought* to have been angry about, but had never *felt* angry about.

When I asked a friend whether or not I should try to get angry about those things, I was shocked to hear these words: "Oh, you already are angry. The question is, what have you done to keep yourself from feeling your anger? And why? What do you stand to lose if you come out of denial about your anger?"

There are no words to describe how unsettling those

questions were to me. I'd prided myself for years on not being angry, because I thought anger was unbecoming to godly women, and all my life I'd wanted to be a godly woman. But the questions would not go away, and for months I struggled to understand the hidden (from myself, at least) parts of my heart.

I had become an expert at stuffing my anger, and God was kind but relentless to expose my strategies for pretending I wasn't angry. I had run from my rage in many ways, most regularly by trying to convince myself things weren't as bad as they seemed, and that what *was* wrong was always my fault, so I had no right to be angry. Minimizing my pain and insisting that I was to blame for everything allowed me to maintain my illusion of control over the events (past and present) that had caused damage to my heart. If I believed I was the one at fault, I could also believe I was powerful enough to somehow change myself and thereby change the way I was being treated. My denial had served to fortify my delusion of omnipotence and had mitigated the impact of my having been betrayed.

Finally, however, as I became willing to acknowledge how angry I was, my anger, though not new, became embarrassingly evident; I simply could not pretend anymore. Then my emotional pendulum began to swing from long-suffering martyrdom to outraged incrimination. I felt justified in blaming Bill for everything that went wrong in my life. To his dismay and matching anger, he became the target against which all my stored-up rage could be deployed. I found myself changing from doormat to shrew in my interactions with him—my accumulated anger in my face and his on a regular basis.

What surprised me, however, was the unsettling sense of pleasure I found in my anger. There was a certain safety in exploding with fury; for some reason the release of my anger felt both satisfying and comforting. The satisfaction, however, seemed illicit and gnawed at my conscience; God was refusing to let me settle down in my anger. Over time He brought me to the realization that my anger, like my earlier denial, was serving the illegitimate function of protecting my heart from the excruciating pain of the harm done to me. I had unconsciously believed that if I entered the pain of men's betrayal, I would either be destroyed or I would destroy others in my rage. Both my denial and my anger toward men were emotional shields fending off the blows I thought would be fatal to my soul.

But God wished to repudiate the lie that was keeping my heart from Himself. He knew if I would enter the pain, and if in the pain I would bring my brokenness to Him, my suffering would unite His heart to mine. I would not become a dangerous woman; on the contrary, I would find the comfort and healing I so desperately needed. And God's Spirit in me would eventually enable me to forgive and bless even those who had done me harm.

This was a suffering I was loathe to embrace, even when I knew I must, because I could not comprehend its redemptive value until after I'd entered and experienced it. How could I have known in those painful months of marital turbulence that genuine hope is only born out of the death of our illusions? Before I could embrace hope, I had to face the reality not only of my anger, but also of my sorrow.

For over three years the saga continued. Not only did I have to learn to grieve my disappointment with Bill, I also had to learn to repent of my self-sufficient attempts to control his life and mine. I faced more misery than I thought I could bear and more sin in myself than I wanted to acknowledge.

What I had not known for most of my life but came to see was that my deepest longing to be cherished could never be fully met by anyone but God. What I had once thought would give me life—the devoted love of a man—was being exposed as the idol it had become. I had much to confess regarding my worship of false gods, and much grace to request and receive from the Father-God who passionately but patiently yearned after my heart.

As I turned to God, I began to experience my heavenly Father as the source of my inner life and my only hope for rest. Though it seems to be a contradiction, the most richly meaningful aspect of those turbulent years with Bill was my eventual brokenness, causing me to hunger desperately for God. "If you do not come to me," I cried out to Him, "I will be undone!"

In the extremities of our helplessness God invites us to turn our hearts toward Him as we embrace the "what is" of our lives. He knows the plans He has for us, and they are plans to prosper us, because He is a good God who longs to be received by us. His redemptive advent to bring us hope in our grieving is the topic of the next chapter.

Recognizing that Reality most vibrantly breaks into hearts that are real in His presence, may we pray for clear insight into what is true about our inner lives, confident that the One who pretends about nothing will lead us with rigorous kindness into the authenticity that will open us to the hope of the gospel.

QUESTIONS FOR REFLECTION AND DISCUSSION
Inviting the Comforter to our side, let us ask Him to show us whatever He deems necessary for the drawing of our hearts closer to Him. Ponder and consider, then, these questions.

1. Without exaggerating the imperfections of your father, brothers, or other key male figures in your childhood, can you put words to what was disappointing to you, as well as what men did to bless your life?
2. What do you fear will happen if you become more honest about your disappointment?
3. How have you minimized the damage men may have done to you?
4. In what ways have you made men pay for the damage they have done to you?
5. How have you refused to give your heart to God or others?
6. How have you shown your contempt toward men?
7. Do your friends experience you as an angry woman?
8. If you were to write a letter to God, expressing your honest feelings about how you have been damaged, what would you say?
9. How do you imagine God would respond to your letter?
10. What does that imagined response reveal about your understanding of who God is and what you think He's like?

CHAPTER FIVE

OUR OPENNESS TOWARD GOD: ENTERING GRIEF

*I don't know any woman of inner beauty who
hasn't suffered greatly and done the hard work
of the gospel that involves grief.*
JODY ENGEL

ew children reared in North America mature into
adulthood without playing the game Hide and Seek. In this
game one player (the seeker) stands at home base with
eyes closed and counts to a prearranged number while
everyone else hides. The seeker then hunts for the hiders,
who try to stay hidden until it's possible to outrun the
seeker to home base.

Eventually even the best hiders are called "home" so a
new game can begin. It's no fair (and no fun) for a hider to
stay hidden. "Get found!" everyone shouts at the hold-outs.
"Come on home!" they call.

And if we have ears to hear, we can recognize in the lan-
guage of those childhood cries the voice of the persistent
Seeker after our painstakingly concealed hearts. "Get
found!" He calls out. "Come on Home!" He invites us all.

For those who will come out of hiding, it is the much
longed for Father-cry of the gospel.

97

OUT OF HIDING

Some of us women have been careful to camouflage what is in our hearts, keeping our truest selves from men, from God, and sometimes even from our own eyes. Fearful that our exposed anger and disappointment would cut us off from the hearts of the men we love and the God we know we cannot live without, many of us hide behind a facade of emotional respectability, pretending all is well—or at least acting as though all is manageable.

But God comes seeking our true hearts, for His own heart is neither taken in nor warmed by our respectable pretense. He wants the real thing, our authentic engagement with Him, even when that means we admit we are angry or upset. "[Because] you are lukewarm—neither hot nor cold—I am about to spit you out of my mouth," said the Living One to the church in Laodicea regarding their lack of spiritual vitality (Revelation 3:16). It is our invitation to authenticity, a call to bring who we really are into His presence to be transformed into renewed intimacy with Him and service for Him by His invigorating gospel of love.

"Get found!" He invites His hiding daughters. "Show Me where you are and I will come to you. Better yet, let Me show you where you are so you can come Home to My love." Our disappointment and anger can open our eyes to what is in our hearts so we can run back to the safe fortress of God's grace.

Some of us, however, once we acknowledge our anger toward fallen men, have trouble getting beyond it. Our anger protects us both from the pain beneath our anger and from our more fundamental disappointment with God. The "safety" of our anger toward men, however, cannot be redemptive, because it keeps us from our deepest need, which is a restored authenticity of relationship with God. For that we must enter our disillusionment not just with men but with the sovereign God who did not prevent us from having been harmed by men.

Hidden beneath even our rage against men and God, often obscured by the intensity of our anger, is a sorrow we hate to enter. In order to understand how to move beyond rage into redemptive sorrow, perhaps an illustration will enable us to see what lies most deeply in our hearts.

FROM RAGE TO SORROW

Not long ago I watched a little girl, maybe two years old, try to control her world from where she sat perched in her mother's grocery cart. She was a beautiful child, blond and adorably dressed, but her eyes and her petulance betrayed her hungry afternoon weariness.

Things fell apart, not surprisingly, in the cereal aisle. She saw the box she wanted, but her mother picked out something more nutritious, and so this otherwise adorable child kicked and screamed and turned bright red. Mama had the advantage of age and experience, however, and her fortunate daughter found she could not hold her mother hostage. Somewhere near the detergent aisle, the child's little-girl rage was reduced to heartbroken sobs, and by the time they reached the produce department her mother could offer her some grapes. She finally fell asleep on her mother's shoulder in the check-out line, and as the bagboy carried out their groceries, I saw this mother turn her face to gently kiss her daughter's resting head.

God calls us to be honest with Him about what is in our hearts—even our anger about the unfairness of what has happened to us as a result of living in a fallen world. We may not be as blatantly uninhibited as that little girl in her tantrum. After all, we as adult women have devised sophisticated ways to hide or redirect our rage so that we'll look good, even to ourselves. But the rage is there, and like the screaming child, we cannot be held by the One who loves us unless we are willing to move beyond the tantrum into heartbreak, and from the heartbreak into partaking of His own sweet grace, which deeply satisfies. Our hearts long for tenderness and rest, but raging children cannot be comforted until they cry. Then their tears can be wiped away, and they can rest and be kissed while they sleep.

Our hearts melt from fury into heartbreak only when we realize we cannot make our lives work on our terms, when we come to see we cannot force anyone to love us the way we know we were meant to be loved—*that* is when we allow ourselves to be broken by our sorrow and go to our heavenly Father for comfort. When we are driven to Him and lay down our rage, then we enter sorrow and can rest in His kind arms.

A STORY OF DUCKS

There is no formula for how or when that will happen. Every woman's story is different, her walk with God like no one else's walk. But consider this small chapter from one woman's story, a tale of how she moved from rage to sorrow because God brought a family of ducks across her path one day in Philadelphia. It happened to my good friend, Penny Freeman. Here's what she told me:

"I learned young how to be hypervigilant and in charge, trying to keep myself safe and my world manageable. But recently God has been undoing my hardheartedness and inviting me to enter both my sorrow about past losses and my longing to rest in Him. Then one day not long ago God exposed my underlying rage at not being able to control my world.

"My husband, John, had invited me to ride in the van with him to run errands, and at a stoplight I looked down and saw a mother duck with about ten newly hatched ducklings in obedient tow, waddling across this busy four-lane road. I let down all my guards of hypervigilance and just really enjoyed the beauty of this mother duck and her babies.

"Of course it takes a while to get those guard-gates up in place again, and suddenly I had a premonition that all was not going to be well for this family of ducks. Before I could find the switch to bring my gates up, the traffic light changed and a red sports car came past on the other side of our van and mowed the ducks down.

"My immediate reaction was total, out-of-control rage. There were tears, but they were tears of fury, not sadness. My irrational anger went first toward John for inviting me to go with him, then toward myself for accepting the invitation, then for letting my guard down, then toward the stupid mother duck for leading her babies across an unsafe highway, then toward the driver of the red sports car (even though he couldn't have seen the ducks in time). Finally my anger spilled out at God for bringing me to a place in my life where I was willing to let my guard down while leaving me in a world where, even though He was in control, He would offer me no guarantee things would always be safe.

"When I saw that my heart was full of rage toward God, He said to me, 'I have known all along how angry you are. I just wanted to let you in on the secret since you seem to be deceived about it.'

"This was clearly, in retrospect, God's invitation to me to repent of my fist in His kind face, but I would have none of it. After my initial rage about the ducks, I went numb for a long time, like I'd done an emotional lobotomy on myself. I simply refused to feel the sadness. It was a wicked response, almost an emotional suicide.

"Finally, when I did repent, I had to be willing to face how I really felt about what had happened that day. God was calling me to weep instead of stay numb. It seems silly that I'm still crying over ducks that died four months ago, but I think my sorrow is more in keeping with who I really am than my wanting to annihilate everybody and everything, including my design to live as a woman impacted by the beauty of a mother duck leading her family.

"I don't always know how to do it, but I know God is calling me to live with the realization that, though I'm not safe, ducks aren't safe, my children aren't safe, He is still a good God. There is no way to protect myself from things being deeply disrupted in my life and experiencing great loss.

"So I'm stuck with the question of what it means to believe God is good even though ducks get killed. And what does it mean to bless my husband in the middle of that scenario, giving him my heart and being vulnerable to sadness instead of protecting myself with my anger? Even though life is not safe, I believe it is sin to be either hypervigilant or numb."

Is it not clear that God can use anything to accomplish His purposes? His invitation to move from rage to sorrow came to Penny in the context of a two-minute experience at a stoplight in Philadelphia, but He will come to no other woman in quite that same way. The question is not, How will He come to us with His invitation to sorrow? but rather, What will we do when He comes?

God's invitation to sorrow is not a once-for-all event, nor is our answer at any given time ever the final word about our hearts. Rather, we find our divine Pursuer searching us out again and again to show us what is in our hearts toward Him. And our repeated movement from rage to sorrow requires that we women journey again and again into our most profound longings. For women who have been shamed for their neediness, it is a most difficult but wonderfully liberating passage.

Our journey is not linear, like a drive through Kansas, but convoluted, like a switchback climb into the Colorado Rockies. We keep passing more or less familiar territory again and again in our uphill trek, but we are closer to the summit each time. More than that, we know God better at every turn in the road at which we allow Him to penetrate our defenses for the larger purpose of bringing us His grace.

GOD IN THE MOURNING

We must understand one thing more about our movement into the sorrow of living without pretense or self-protection in a bent world. It is this: When we relinquish our rage and the control strategies that have been fueled by that rage, we enter life with God and men on a new plane, one that will feel uncomfortable to us for a time. Our old assumptions about life, about godliness, about what it means to be a woman will be challenged, and we will have to learn to live in the discomfort of being loved beyond any hope of controlling or managing that love. We will also be asked to feel our pain instead of run from it, to embrace our grief instead of mask or drown it. That is our unlikely route to joy, for if we hide from the sorrow our relationships may have caused us (and may continue to cause us), we are likely to miss the rich tastes of gladness those relationships can offer us as well.

My friend Jody Engel described this new way of living by giving words to her own experience, saying, "For most of my life I would not grieve, because it was seen as a weakness: Strong women don't grieve. Now I believe *only* strong women can grieve, and it's a weakness *not* to grieve. The call to sadness is not a popular one, but it is a kind one, because if we won't grieve, how can we be comforted? I don't think Jesus named the Holy Spirit the Comforter just on a whim. He wasn't pretending this was easy. He knew. He told us. We just chose not to believe Him, and that is our own lie and our own loss.

"Jesus suffered," Jody continued, "and He invites us to suffer, too. I think to suffer well is to be sad and not pretend, knowing we won't be destroyed by our disappointment because God will keep our souls intact. We find it easy to give God our list of demands regarding our circumstances, but will we go to Him with the brokenness of our hearts? God has a penchant for brokenness. It was only when Jacob's hip was out of joint that he asked God for the blessing. We refuse to be broken before God, yet that is all He requires of us."

Though we hate the helplessness of heartbreak, God calls us to put down our weapons of rage and enter our sadness. *Sorrow* is not a comfortable word; *brokenness* is even worse. But God's comforting Spirit is sent not to the self-sufficient, but to those who mourn the little and large losses in life. A broken and contrite heart He never shames.

Grieving, in fact, is a necessary part of learning to live the way Christ lived in the world. Surely He savored tastes of delighting in His Father's good gifts—celebrating weddings and enjoying dinner parties in His honor and holding little children on His lap. But He was also "despised and rejected by men, a man of sorrows, and familiar with suffering"

(Isaiah 53:3). He struggled to endure the recurring opposition of the Pharisees, the disbelief of His own family and
intimate disciples, and the wicked manhandling of the San-
hedrin and the Roman guard—to name just some aspects of
His sorrowing. Luci Shaw rightly said, "The suffering of
Christ was not limited to what He endured on the cross, but
included all that He experienced as a result of the Incarnation. And when we enter our own suffering, there is a closeness to Christ and an identification with Him that I think
moves God's own heart. If we won't 'die' by being willing to
suffer, we won't live either—it's like the seed falling into the
gound in order to germinate into new life."

Luci went on to say, "Even our ambivalence and uncertainty open us up to the grace of God. But facing our frailty
is the hardest thing we do, and we often shield ourselves
against it. To live by faith is to live as though God is there,
even when we're not always sure He is."

And that is exactly when God comes in a particularly
intimate way—at those times when we're not sure He's
there, yet we are willing to live as though He is. When we
refuse to go *around* our sorrow and instead walk into and
through it, trusting to find God there, that is when we taste
a closeness with Him we never knew we could experience.
Susan Yates, an author and pastor's wife from Falls Church,
Virginia, said this about a friend whose husband is not a
believer: "Even though it's lonely and painful for her, God is
there in the midst of her pain, and she has seen the hand of
God in her life and has grown in her walk with the Lord in
ways she probably never would have grown otherwise. Pain is
where God is in His glory, because He knows pain. Unbe-
lievers go through dark pain, a pain that is a black hole, but
the believer's pain is wrapped up with the glow of the presence of Christ." And it is His presence that offers us joy in
our sorrow.

But it is not merely the presence of God in our pain that
redeems our sorrow. It is what God is able to do in the midst
of our sorrow to change our hearts. That is what showcases

God's glory to the world and confounds the evil intentions of God's enemy. We must never forget who our real enemy is—not men, not our easily seduced flesh, certainly not God, though these are what we are most likely to engage in battle. Our true enemy is the one who is unremitting in his efforts to destroy our souls, often using human tools to implement his diabolical schemes.

When we as women enter the truth about our lives, we can also embrace the higher purpose of knowing God in a way that will thwart Satan's evil intentions to destroy our souls. Thus will the victory won on Calvary accomplish God's ultimate plan to turn all things to our good if we devote our hearts to being conformed to Our Savior's likeness (Romans 8:28-29).

TRIUMPH OVER TRAGEDY
"For most of my life I was not aware that anything bad had been done to me," confided the pastor's wife sitting across from me at her kitchen table. "I thought it was all normal. But I was asked one time to counsel a girl who was a victim of sexual abuse, and someone gave me a book about abuse to prepare me for my time with her.

"Well," she went on to say, "I almost broke my hand. I was sitting in the bathtub reading that book and I didn't even realize I was pounding my fist on the wall, crying my eyes out. I had all the symptoms of having been abused myself, every one of the classic symptoms."

Shaking her head, she lamented, "Our generation has been so defiled. I've been struggling with the results of my abuse for many years, trying to deal with its impact on my life. I can't fix it, of course. Only a sovereign God working sovereignly can give me what I need."

This courageous woman's conclusion was as wise as her story was disconcerting. Jan Frank, who wrote the book *Door of Hope* about sexual abuse, put words to our sure hope when she said, "The very thing Satan intended for our destruction God intends for our good. When I speak to women about childhood sexual abuse, I tell them that facing our abuse experiences is not ultimately about damage but about redemption, about knowing God. All the things He brings us through are not for the sake of the event, but for the sake of knowing Him and seeing His power to redeem the unredeemable.

"It was no accident I grew up in the family I did, even though much damage was done to me there," Jan told me. "Because of what God did in me as I faced that damage, my experience has become a demonstration of His power."

Isn't that just like God? He takes the damage Satan meant to use to overthrow our lives and by His presence within our brokenness and sorrow He transforms our wounded hearts into trophies of His grace and power. We are profoundly changed in His presence, because in our sorrow and rest in Him we find the deep intimacy we were created to enjoy, and we are made whole.

That is His glory and our rich gain!

GOD'S NATURE REVEALED

As we pursue our journey into hope by embracing authenticity regarding our relationships, we must not forget the most important question of all: What is happening in that most foundational of all relationships, our intimacy with God? We know we cannot love Him as we ought, but our deeper struggle is to believe He loves us as much as we need to be loved. Even beyond the integrity of entering our own honest emotions, we must face what God has revealed in Scripture regarding His own feelings toward us, His image-bearers.

Our emotional life, though corrupted by sin, nevertheless reflects a God who does not hesitate to communicate His own strong sentiments toward those He loves. He is never portrayed as dispassionate toward His people. When the Israelites abandoned Him for other gods, His words to the prophet Hosea, whose wife had prostituted herself, were words about God's own fierce love for His adulterous people: "Go, show your love to your wife again," God said to Hosea, "though she is loved by another and is an adulteress. Love her as the LORD loves the Israelites, though they turn to other gods and love the sacred raisin cakes" (3:1). God would send His beloved people into exile for their sin, but His heart was broken by it: "How can I hand you over, Israel?" He lamented; "all my compassion is aroused" (11:8).

These words do not suggest that God is an impersonal, aloof Prime Initiator who wound up the universe like a clock and left it to run itself down while He stands by curious but uninvolved. Rather, these are the words of a betrayed lover whose emotions are on a roller-coaster ride. God was not benevolently disinterested in His people's hearts; He was angry, brokenhearted, jealous, and enraptured all at once.

And what about Jesus? Scripture teaches that He was frustrated with His disciples' disbelief when He descended the Mount of Transfiguration, sad at Lazarus's grave site, and angrily upset in the temple marketplace. Surely He struggled with the pain and perplexity of life. Was His inner life orderly in the Garden of Gethsemane as He grappled with the stark reality of His approaching abuse and death? Did the blood of His struggle on the ground of that garden show evidence of sin in Him?

If Jehovah in the Old Testament and Jesus in the New Testament displayed strong emotions in relating to our finite ways of perceiving who God is, we bear His image most accurately when we, too, attend and give voice to what we feel, especially regarding our relationships. We are invited to enter with courage the reality of what is in our hearts, for in this we imitate not only the example of God's people, whose words about Him and to Him were startlingly honest, but the example of God Himself, whose feelings toward His people were invariably clear.

God is both the giver and receiver of words, for words expose the heart. When we give words to what we feel, we reflect the relational nature of God who speaks first to us and receives our words in response because He longs for connectedness with us. That is who He is and what He is like.

The psalmist David was inviting God's heart connection with him when he cried out,

> Search me, O God, and know my heart;
>   test me and know my anxious thoughts.
> See if there is any offensive way in me,
>   and lead me in the way everlasting.
>   (Psalm 139:23-24)

Why would David do such a dangerous thing as to ask God to expose "any offensive way" in his heart? Is it not because he was willing to face whatever God revealed to him about his heart, for the larger purpose of knowing God better and loving Him more deeply? We, too, are invited to interactive openness with God regarding how we really feel, even when what we feel is anger or frustration. We are called to be like the psalmists, not just to acknowledge but to give voice to what we are feeling. For only in that way can we be real with ourselves and with the God who longs for our true hearts, not our religious performance. Facing our emotions will lead us into what is real, and because God is the ultimate Reality, it is there we will find Him and taste His presence.

OUR HEARTS TOWARD GOD

It was so with me. The turmoil Bill and I experienced in our marriage was a summons into reality, exposing the anger that had been in my heart toward Bill and toward many other men who had done me harm. God had much to teach me regarding my strategies for denying that anger and for staying out of pain and in control, strategies that had kept me distant not only from the men who occupied my life, but also from God Himself.

Even more devastating, though, was my unwillingness to admit what was most deeply in my heart toward God. When I acknowledged my anger and looked at my losses, I also had to admit I was enraged at God for not having protected me well, and for not having rewarded my efforts to be a godly woman by giving me a loving husband and a happy marriage. It is true what Drs. Allender and Longman said in their book, *Cry of the Soul:* "[We] are to listen to and ponder what we feel in order to be moved to the far deeper issue of what our hearts are doing with God and others."[1] When I could no longer pretend about how disappointing my marriage was, I could also no longer pretend I wasn't furious with God for allowing me to enter such an unhappy situation. When I stopped denying the truth about my inner life, I also came out of denial regarding the angry fist I brandished in God's face on a regular basis.

And that, amazingly enough, is where God came to me most intimately—not in my polished perfectionism, not in my pretense, not even most deeply in my suffering, but in my admission that I was enraged with Him and thought I had every right *not* to believe in His goodness. "Why should I trust You?" was the question I flung at Him. "How can I believe in Your goodness when I look at the bad things that have happened to me?"

Jesus came to me at that point and He did an amazing thing. Instead of damning me for my blasphemy against His character (which damnation I most surely deserved), He showed me His hands. No chiding. No words at all. Just the up-turning of His pierced palms in an unspoken invitation to recognize and receive the evidence of His love and to believe it was for me. When I entered the awful reality of my soul, Reality Himself ushered me anew into the wonder of the gospel of grace. And I worshiped.

CANDOR AND GOD'S PRESENCE
Grace is like that. When we least expect it (because we least deserve it), it dawns on us in ways we cannot comprehend. God comes to us in our honesty in ways He cannot break through when we pretend about what is really in our hearts. In the face of all our attempts to polish the exterior of our lives, to look godly and to appear spiritually mature, it seems

God has a preference for our hearts, tainted though they are with sin and self-centeredness.

God does not fear our anger, even when it is misdirected toward Him. His love is large enough to encircle us and draw us to Himself, even with our fists flailing. When we come to Him with our honesty, He is ready to do what He must—comfort us in our pain, confront us with our sin, or enjoy our longing to love Him more passionately—and sometimes all three at once. When we open our eyes to see what is really going on in our hearts, He stands ready to receive us if we will receive His grace.

When we enter the reality of any of our feelings, we are in a position to see what we most deeply believe about God. When we stop pretending about our anger at the loss of what we were created to enjoy, we gain a window on whether the movement of our hearts in response to our pain has been to try to control God and others or to rest in God's goodness. The disappointment we experience when we face how men may have harmed us as women creates fissures in our souls that will either be deepened by our fury or healed by our grieving. If we will take the time to mourn our losses, we will find the perseverance to wait until God comes.

Rage or sorrow—where do we most often live? God is willing to show us, but it requires that we stop running from our pain, particularly the pain that comes from the broken relationships in our lives, past and present. If we want to know God deeply—to know both our own hearts toward Him and His toward us—we must be willing to look even beneath our surface anger and face our losses. Pat Palau said, regarding the feminine anger so prevalent in our society today, "I'm inclined to believe that behind every angry woman is an incredibly bleak and barren relationship with some man." I think she is right. The question is, are we willing to look at and grieve over the barren relationships that lie beneath our anger?

Herein lies our hope. God will not leave us desolate; He will be there with us as we face our disappointment and loss.

And because we will surely find Him there, His presence is sure to expose our hidden rage and then invite us to find our rest in Him—if not all at once, at least incrementally. As we rest in Him, embracing our sorrow instead of indulging our rage, He will also bring us to a kinder, more genuine love for others, especially the men in our lives. Even, perhaps, the men who have done us harm. Nothing is too hard for God, and there is every reason to be encouraged in our hope in Him. We can hope to love even imperfect men well because of His presence in our sorrow.

We long to enter that hope, but we wonder how we can love fallen men in a way that neither ignores their sin nor holds their sin irrevocably against them. The path is not easy, but it is richly rewarding. The next chapter will explore one primary step along that path.

———◦◦◦———

With faith that we can come to know our wonderful God ever more intimately, may we risk the lowering of our fists so we can receive both the love-filled eyes and tender embrace of the One who sorrows at our rage and invites us to do likewise.

———◦◦◦———

QUESTIONS FOR REFLECTION AND DISCUSSION
As we live in the midst of sorrow and hope in our relationships, perhaps our most vital concern must be our willingness to engage with God in a way that is both authentic and
worshipful. With that goal in mind, consider the following
questions.

1. What has God revealed about Himself in your angry
   moments with Him?
2. What tastes has He offered you of resting in Him in the
   midst of your sorrow?
3. What keeps you from loving God without reserve?
4. What would change in your life if you really believed
   God loves you without reserve?
5. What do you fear God will expose in you if you invite
   Him, as David did, to search your heart?
6. What would God do with what He knows about your
   heart?
7. Do you really want God to know you that intimately?
8. How do you hope God will deal with you if you become
   more candid?
9. Do you most regularly live in rage or in sorrow about
   your losses? Explain.
10. What might happen if you changed that choice?

CHAPTER SIX

OUR HOPE IN GOD: RELINQUISHING CONTROL

God promises He won't leave us,
but He doesn't promise us easy lives.
VALERIE BELL

*M*argie Cooper was an amazing woman. Stricken with polio in 1945 and confined to an iron lung for forty years, she lived with incredible courage, resilient faith, and a wonderfully cheerful nature.

But just as amazing was her husband, John, as described by their son, the Reverend Dale Cooper, chaplain at Calvin College in Grand Rapids, Michigan.

"When Mom got sick," Dale recalled, "Dad kept magnificently the expensive vows he had made to her. Every morning he lifted her from the iron lung and gave her daily care, washing her, brushing her teeth, and combing her hair. He was the hands by which she did things: he shopped, cleaned house, fed her, switched on the television, even turned the pages in books or magazines.

"These things Dad did uncomplainingly, as though it were no big deal. When an unbeliever once expressed astonishment that he would stay with a woman who had so little left to offer, Dad declared the gospel with eloquence, saying, 'I love my wife. I'm a Christian and we try to keep our promises.'

"My father," Dale concluded, "left me a wonderful legacy of kept vows and selfless love. I count it a privilege to bear his name."[1]

The impressive thing is not just the devoted care-giving of John Cooper, but the equally costly care-accepting of his wife, Margie. For her to live so utterly unmanageable an existence for forty years, she had to learn the grace of accepting with cheerfulness a total relinquishment of control. What did she know of God that kept her from becoming bitter in her helplessness?

THE COMPULSION TO CONTROL
Part of the answer, of course, is that it is our very experience of feeling out of control that invites us to know and trust God more. Mary Farrar, an author and conference speaker residing in Dallas, Texas, told me about her struggle with severe burnout during her early years of campus ministry, and she concluded with these wise words: "Sometimes when we go through really hard times and come to the end of our rope, we taste God's faithfulness firsthand, and we can see how He uses that experience to significantly strengthen our relationship with Him."

Mary was right. But it is difficult for us to admit we've come to the end of our rope, especially in terms of our relationships, especially our relationships with men. Control is always an issue for us.

Our need to manage the men in our lives is primarily about our aloneness. We move to control men in order to procure for ourselves the relationships we think we cannot live without. Our inclination toward relational manipulation is revealed in Scripture as early as Genesis 3.

When God came looking for His disobedient children

after their fall from grace, He spoke gospel words to them, but He also spoke words of judgment. What He named for Eve as the consequence for her sin was distress in the two areas about which women are most naturally concerned: "I will greatly increase your pains in childbearing," God said, then added, "Your desire will be for your husband, and he will rule over you" (3:16). Thus, in our primary relationships as mothers and wives, we as Eve's daughters receive God's blessing as we connect with men and bear their children, but we also know physical pain in giving birth and relational pain in dealing with men who do not always move toward us for our good.

Pain in childbirth surely addresses what is intrinsically feminine in us, namely, our ability and longing to bear and nurture children. Barbara Feil, women's ministry leader and part-time professor at Multnomah Bible College, said, "My own childlessness has made me very aware that not all women are mothers, but I've always considered the most profound scriptural truth about the roles of men and women to be that women have the babies." Our femininity is confirmed when we are with child.

But what did God mean when He told Eve, "Your desire will be for your husband"? To better understand the word *desire,* consider how the word is used in the story of Cain and Abel found in Genesis 4. There we read of Cain's anger because the Lord had looked with favor on Abel's offering but not his own. God came to Cain and graciously invited him to face what was in his heart that kept him from enjoying God's favor, warning him, "If you do not do what is right, sin is crouching at your door; *it desires to have you,* but you must master it" (Genesis 4:7, emphasis added).

God had said to Eve, "Your *desire* will be for your husband." He said to Cain, "[Sin] *desires* to have you." They are the same word, but how are the sentences alike, and why did God put them in such immediate proximity to one another?

If we think of *desire* in the context of being image-bearers of a relational, Triune God, then desiring somebody is a good thing in that it reflects God's desire for connectedness with us. His divine longing for our hearts is always for our good, always intent on blessing, always redemptive, always life-bringing. Our first parents, created to image God, desired one another for mutual blessing and enjoyment.

That all changed, however, after their fall into disobedience. When God addresses the woman's desire for her husband *outside* the context of perfectly imaging God's own selfless love, her desire is tainted in two ways. First, the energy of her desire was no longer other-centered, but self-centered. No longer would she long for Adam in order to receive and bless him with her responsiveness; now she would desire that he meet *her* needs for love.

In addition to tainting Eve's motives, the Fall also depraved her method for getting what she desired. No longer would she invite her husband to come to her; she would try to somehow *make* him come to her. Her movement would be to control and possess him—to "desire to *have*" him, as Satan desired to *have* and control Cain's heart. That feminine inclination to possess and control men has contaminated Eve's daughters ever since.

And what of Adam's "rule over" his wife? His heart movement, too, would be tainted by self-centeredness. Irresistibly drawn to her because of his God-imaging relational nature, as a fallen man he would now be inclined to use his initiatory strength for selfish ends, ruling not as Christ shepherds the Church with sacrificial love but as "the rulers of the Gentiles lord it over" their subjects (Matthew 20:25). Instead of moving to bless, he would move to dominate, and dominated women "lose sight of whatever dreams they once dared to dream," as my sister, Mary Swierenga, so aptly said.

The only way any of us can experience love is to receive it, not demand it. Men's movement toward us must be their free choice, even as our responsiveness to their love must be our free choice. In both of these—the free giving and the joyous receiving of love—we live out the image of God's love within the Trinity.

How kind of God to show us in such an immediate juxtaposition of the word *desire* in Genesis 3 and 4 the terrible consequence of our wrongly directed feminine desire: If we move to control or "own" with our desire, we end up at the mercy of that desire. And as surely as Satan's desire for Cain's heart ended in Abel's murder, so the result of our compulsion to control is always the death of our relationships as they were meant to be. Better that we by God's grace and enabling should master our compulsion to control than that we be mastered by it.

RELINQUISHING CONTROL

God calls us to master our tendency to try to manipulate men, but it will not be easy. We will have to stop demanding that they never let us down and instead learn to live with inviting hands instead of threatening fists. But how can we come to desire men without controlling or consuming them?

To state the solution to our dilemma most simply, we as women cannot love men with an openness to both their love gifts and their love failures without a radical dependence on God. We must remember that our relationships with men always and fundamentally bring us back to questions regarding our relationship with God. Our attempts to control men mirror our strategies for controlling God. Our anger toward men for not coming to our hearts flows from our anger at God for not coming to our rescue.

We must struggle through our uncertainty regarding the character of God and come to call Him *good* in designing us for relationships with men, even though our connection with them may have caused us pain or shame. God is not unkind to ask that we give men not only our hands or our competence or our minds or even our bodies, but our hearts as well. We may think God cruel to leave us longing for men in a broken world where there is no guarantee of safety for our hearts. But cruelty is utterly inconsistent with who God has revealed Himself to be.

Questions regarding God's nature have profound implications for how we live in relationship with men—not just
husbands, but fathers and brothers and friends as well. What
we do with our hearts toward them depends on what we
believe in our hearts about God. If God is good and His
design for us is right, then we are wrong to kill our longings
or to pretend we don't love and desire relationships with
good men.

Our feminine struggle to affirm the good character of
God runs deepest when we have not tasted or are not
presently tasting the relational gifts He designed us to
receive—men's kind words and tender affection and pro-
tective strength exercised for our good. And that struggle
offers us all, single or married, the choice between bitterness or sorrow.

The struggle also calls us to something even more difficult as women. If we have grappled with whether God is *good*
in designing us to long for men, even when they are unavailable, the deeper question is whether in the midst of our sorrow over our relational losses, God is *enough* for us. Even
though we can't make men come to us with their hearts or
change their behavior toward us, we must trust God enough
to let go of our control strategies regarding men. We must
give up trying to make men come to us or make them
change. We must live out of the reality that *God* is our life,
not the men He does or does not bring to us.

More than that, if we do give up the control devices by
which we strive to connect with men, our call is to love even
those who are not giving us what God intended them to give
us, endeavoring prayerfully to understand what that kind of
love would look like.

A word of caution is worth repeating: When the relationship between a man and a woman is abusive, the most
loving thing is to address the sin that is keeping God's trini-
tarian image from being revealed in that relationship. When
women fail to respect men or when men harm women (physically, sexually, or verbally), the reflection of God's charac-

ter is obscured. A woman who ignores or minimizes the damage done to her by a man is failing to love him. We do not show godly respect to men when we allow our fear to keep us from confronting their sin. Their sin devastates their masculine souls as surely as it harms our own hearts or bodies.

Sin is not neutral, nor is God neutral about it. Both our own disrespect toward men (through silence or shrewishness) and men's mistreatment of women (through hardheartedness or abandonment) are detestable to God. God's steady love is relentless to cut away the cancer of sin that threatens our spiritual health, and we cooperate with His hatred of sin when we confront it in ourselves or others.

This means that we continually bring our own motives and actions before the piercing gaze of God's Spirit and His Word so we can repent and receive forgiveness for whatever sin He shows us. We cannot repent for anyone else's sin, of course, but we are not wrong to name it and to refuse to condone it. In showing men the harm their sin does us, we offer them opportunity to take a look at their hearts toward us and toward God. In our confronting, as in our waiting, it is God alone who must be both stronghold for our hearts and the source of our energy to love with boldness the fallen men against whose sin we firmly take our stand.

Clearly, we cannot relinquish our attempts to control men and learn to love them well without a radical dependence on God. Perhaps it is time we ask ourselves what that would call forth in us and how we can come to experience it.

RELATIONSHIPS THAT BEAR FRUIT

Sarah, Abraham's wife, is a good example of how to live with a vibrant confidence in God. The Apostle Peter considered her life worthy of our admiration and imitation, commending her inner beauty displayed in her responsiveness to her husband's initiation and covering (1 Peter 3:1-6). We have much to learn from her story regarding our own dependence on God.

Sarah wanted what the daughters of Eve have always

longed to enjoy: a relationship with a man that would bear fruit. Thus Sarah was a true daughter of Eve in that she longed for both a husband who would not let her down and a child who would be the fruit of their union. In both of these, Sarah was disappointed.

We read of Sarah's barrenness even before we read about God's call to Abram (Genesis 11:30). But it doesn't take long before we also read of her disillusionment with her husband, who moved temporarily from Canaan to Egypt to avoid a famine. "As he was about to enter Egypt," Scripture tells us, "he said to his wife Sarai, 'I know what a beautiful woman you are. When the Egyptians see you, they will say, "This is his wife." Then they will kill me but will let you live. Say you are my sister, so that I will be treated well for your sake and my life will be spared because of you'" (Genesis 12:11-13).

It was a convenient ploy on Abram's part and only partially untrue; Sarai was his half-sister, daughter of his father but not of his mother (see 20:12). But his plan for self-protection not only exposed his lack of faith in God, it also exposed his wife to shame and dishonor when his plan backfired and Sarai was taken into Pharaoh's court to be readied for his harem (12:14-16). Given this horrifying turn of events, how could she ever again trust in Abram as a safe man?

Whatever else Sarai experienced there in the palace of a powerful and wicked king, the Apostle Peter says she learned the most important lesson of all: she learned to put her hope in God (1 Peter 3:5)—not in her husband nor her own beauty nor her own wit, but in the only One who could redeem her life. And her hope was not disappointed, for "the LORD inflicted serious diseases on Pharaoh and his household because of Abram's wife Sarai." In response, Pharaoh returned Sarai to her husband, sending him away with all he had acquired because of her beauty (Genesis 12:17-20). And so Sarai was saved, not because of Abram but in spite of him.

Surely Sarai's trust in Abram as a good man was as shaken as her trust in God was strengthened by that experience in Egypt. But she was still left with the sorrow of not having a relationship with a man that would bear fruit; she remained barren. For over a decade Sarai waited for God to intervene in her tent as He had intervened in Pharaoh's palace, until finally she felt she could wait no longer.

Unwilling to go on hoping in God's promise and timing, she tried to remedy her barrenness and make *herself* fruitful. Going to Abram, she said, "The LORD has kept me from having children. Go, sleep with my maidservant; perhaps I can build a family through her" (Genesis 16:2). Do you hear the incongruity in her words? *I* can build a family, she said, forgetting not only that it is in the union of two that a family is built, but even more fundamentally that God had promised Abram that *He* would build Abram's family (12:2). It was a most disastrous and altogether unsuccessful remedy.

Are we not all daughters of Sarai, even as we are all daughters of Eve? When we are frustrated at the apparent unfruitfulness of trusting in God, do we not attempt to build our future, taking things into our own hands to force God to give us what we want? God didn't stop Sarai, nor does He always keep us from our foolishness. For thirteen years Sarai bore the consequences of her attempt to control her own life as she watched Ishmael, the fruit of Abram's intimacy with Hagar, grow to adolescence among her desert tents.

But at last God announced to Abraham in Sarah's presence that she would bear a child at the outrageous age of ninety (Genesis 18:10). Scripture records her response: "So Sarah laughed to herself as she thought, 'After I am worn out and my master is old, will I now have this pleasure?'" (18:12)

This was indeed a test of Sarah's faith. She would have to allow herself, an old woman, to long for intimacy with her husband, believing against all reason that her coming together with Abraham, an imperfect and an *old* man, would bear fruit. Sarah was invited to know pleasure unto laughter, the pleasure of intimacy that would produce the child of promise whose name, Isaac, means "laughter." And in the fruitfulness of that union, Sarah would know in a deeper way that though a pregnant senior citizen was surely a laughable absurdity, she was not a fool to have put her hope in God.

A CHOICE OF THE HEART

How gracious of God to give us Sarah's story as an encouragement to those who long for godliness! "You are [Sarah's] daughters," the Apostle Peter reminds us, "if you do what is right and do not give way to fear" (1 Peter 3:6). He does not tell us never to be afraid; he just urges us to "not give way" to doing what our fearful hearts tempt us to do to take control of our lives.

Sarah's husband, Abraham, gives us further encouragement to trust God for what is most important to us. Abraham was a true son of Adam, whose punishment for his sin in the Garden of Eden was directed not so much toward his longing for relationships that would bear fruit as toward his longing for soil that would bear fruit—that is, fruitful labor.

"Cursed is the ground because of you," God had said to Adam; "through painful toil you will eat of it all the days of your life. It will produce thorns and thistles for you" (Genesis 3:17-18). Just as women would struggle primarily with the futility of unfruitful relationships (relationships they can't seem to make "work"), so men would struggle first and foremost with the futility of unfruitful soil (work that is hard and that often seems meaningless or hopeless).

Consider Abraham. God had promised that he would become a great nation, bringing him to the land his descendants would one day inherit. But at the age of 100, though Abraham had accumulated much wealth, he owned no real estate in Canaan and had only one son of the promise, Isaac. The meaning of his existence hinged on that one child, the only evidence God would fulfill His promise to make Abraham's life fruitful.

Because God wants to be first in our hearts, He sometimes offers us opportunities to reveal the depth of our faith in Him. Though Abraham had exposed the weakness of his faith regarding God's sovereignty in the earlier matter of

Sarai and Pharaoh, God in His kindness offered him another opportunity to see what was in his heart.

"Take your son," God one day said to Abraham, "your only son, Isaac, whom you love, and go to the region of Moriah. Sacrifice him there as a burnt offering on one of the mountains I will tell you about" (Genesis 22:2). No explanation (with which Abraham could argue). No hint that Abraham was wrong to love Isaac (so repentance wouldn't help). No reason to hope for a reprieve (even a plea for mercy wasn't an option). Just a choice to be made: Obey God or cling to his son. When Abraham arrived at the killing place on the sacred mountain, he built an altar, bound his beloved son, and raised his knife for the death blow that would answer the most fundamental question of his existence: *Is life found in God or in my son, Isaac?*

But God stayed Abraham's hand and provided a ram, caught in a thicket nearby, to take Isaac's place on the sacrificial altar. When God calls us to worship, He always provides the means to do so. He did it for Abraham, and He did it again at that later Moriah altar, the cross of Calvary, where He did not stay His own Son-slaughtering hand. What He had kept Abraham from doing, He Himself did for our sakes.

Finally the promise is reiterated to Abraham, God's man. Because of his dogged faith in God's goodness (which must have seem obscured by the monstrous act God had asked of him), and because of the obedience that flowed out of his heart of faith, God would *surely* do for Abraham what He had already promised He would do. Because Abraham was willing to trust God with the outcome of his obedience, the meaning of his life was redeemed from futility to fruitfulness.

INDIVIDUAL STRUGGLES
It seems significant that Sarah is nowhere mentioned in the story of Abraham's Moriah experience. She may not even have known that Abraham had left their tent with death on his mind toward Isaac. There is no record that she was either

informed or consulted regarding her husband's struggle and her son's jeopardy.

Perhaps the reason for her noninvolvement lies in the fact that, though God carries out His plans in the context of community (the Old Testament nation of Israel and the New Testament Church), He conducts His relationships with His image-bearers on an individual level. The story of Abraham's battle to relinquish his son is the story of one man's private wrestling match with the God of the universe. God had far-ranging plans for His nation and His church when He came to Abraham, but He was pleased to carry out those plans in the setting of His intimate friendship with this one man. That is always how He works—His large plans emerging out of the overflow of His relationship with individual image-bearers. Our lives are part of a much broader picture than we can presently see.

In the intimacy of individually calling Abraham to live out of a heart fully devoted to Him, God put His finger on what Abraham cherished most—the son through whom God's promise of a fruitful life would be fulfilled. Isaac was an integral part of the lives of both his parents, but the meaning of Abraham's existence was embodied in Isaac in a way that was fundamentally different from Sarah's love for Isaac as the fruit of her relationship with Abraham.

Sarah had engaged in her own personal contest to know her heart as fully devoted to God, but her battle was about the relational fruitfulness she longed to enjoy. Her struggle to give her life into God's hands took place in her tent at Hebron, and she had lost one skirmish of faith when she offered her maidservant to Abraham. But she won a second round when she received God's gift of a child from Abraham at the age of eighty-nine in that same family tent. Sarah's struggle in Hebron was not the same as Abraham's on Moriah, though both struggles exposed their individual hearts toward God—hers in the area of relationships, his related to his work in the world.

This difference is significant for two reasons. First, we

must recognize that we as women cannot fight men's battles for them. Sarah did not figure prominently (if at all) in Abraham's Moriah battle because it was never intended to be her battle. In fact, the battle wasn't even about Isaac; it was about Abraham and God. It was for God and God alone that Abraham walked up that desolate, holy mountain, his knife intent on obedience. He could slay his son because he believed God is good. It was not that he loved the boy less, but that he loved this wild, untamable, holy Presence more. His trembling hand was sure because he believed God's word was sure and was surety for his life. The death of his son would not be the death of him, grievous though the loss would be. This Abraham knew because he had grappled with God in a way Sarah could not have entered into with him.

We, too, must keep our feminine wiles out of the battles our men wage with God. We sometimes think it is our job to fix or manage or force or protect our men in their walk with God. But God wants us to realize that He will fight "man-to-man" with them in ways He does not engage with us as women. He knows which battles to fight with each man—He invited Abraham to sacrifice his son, but He wrestled hand-to-hand with Abraham's grandson, Jacob. Why the difference? Only God knows, because He alone knows each man's unique heart. And we as women must trust Him to fight wisely and cleanly and at just the right time with our men, taking care to stay out of the fray ourselves.

A second reason to highlight the difference between God's struggles with His sons and with His daughters centers on our tendency to expect men to be concerned about relationships in the same way we are. God surely designed men for connectedness with Himself and with us, but it is not the same as our longing for heart-to-heart ties with our families and friends. Men have their own boxing matches to fight with God, but those contests may not even have to do with their relationships with us as their wives or sisters or daughters or friends, and that is not necessarily evidence of sin in them.

Sarah struggled in Hebron. Abraham went to Moriah.

Both responded individually to God's penetrating challenge: "Will you take whatever you think you cannot live without and sacrifice it to me? Will you sign its death warrant with no guarantee of my sovereign reprieve?" Neither God's sons nor His daughters can find rest in God's love except to the degree we give up our idols, recognizing that connectedness to Him is the point of everything. Christ is our life—not a man or a child or a friend or a job or financial security or control or marriage, but intimate relationship with and knowledge of the One who has redeemed us from death.

When we believe our relationship with God is our greatest priority, He will fulfill men's masculine desire for work that matters and our own longing for personal intimacy—but these will be *side-benefits* of His own coming to us. Restored relationship with God is *life;* the potential for fruitful labor or relationships with good men is the *overflow* of God's life in us. God may or may not give us the meaningful jobs or the good husbands He intends us to desire, but He calls us always to preserve our priorities: Relationship with Him is primary, and our success or our good relationships are at His discretion.

THE BILTMORE BATTLE

All of us have idols we love more than God. The real question is whether or not, when He exposes them to us, we will relinquish them as an act of loyalty to Him. God's exposure of my idolatry did not happen in the way or at a time I expected. I'd been struggling in my marriage with Bill for some time when God confronted me with the divine interrogatory: "What do you count most dear, My daughter—your needs as a woman or My plan for you? Am I enough in your desert of loneliness? Can you love Me and can you love this man out of your aridness?"

I had come to the point in my relationship with Bill where nothing I said or did made any difference—he simply would not change. I had pulled out all the stops for more than three years—crying, sulking, shouting, threatening, cajoling, withdrawing, withholding, forgiving, confronting, praying with, praying for, praying against, praying about, practicing tough love, issuing ultimatums, retracting them, offering compromises—whatever I thought would work to save my marriage and win Bill's heart back. Finally, at the end of my rope, I checked into the elegant Biltmore Hotel in Coral Gables, Florida, for a three-day weekend alone, telling myself and my closest friends I just couldn't go on living that way anymore. I needed to make a decision about what to do with the rest of my life.

It was a beautiful room, tastefully decorated and blessedly silent. For three days I ordered room service, took naps, cried, went for walks, thought about how I would ask Bill for a separation, and wondered what would happen to our teenage son. I mentally divided our furniture, worked the crossword puzzles in the newspapers delivered free to my room, tried to listen to God's voice, and dreamed of finally being out from under the pressure and unremitting pain I'd been living in for what seemed like decades. *I can't go on*, I kept saying to myself. *Surely God can't expect me to keep living this way.*

Then God spoke.

I had called a friend, and she was asking me what I was planning to do. "I want to ask Bill for a separation," I replied.

"What will happen if you do that?" she pursued.

"He will probably divorce me," I acknowledged.

Then these words from her mouth: "You know, of course, that you don't have grounds for a divorce."

Stunned silence on my part. The words may have come out of her mouth, but they were God's words as if He had taken the telephone from her and spoken them with His own voice, so piercingly did they penetrate my sorrowing heart.

With a clarity I could neither deny nor evade, God had tolled the death knell to my hope for escape. I would go home. I would go on struggling to love a man who would not bend his knee to God nor give his heart to me. I would take the knife I had poised over my marriage and put it in the

Father's hand. I would rest in Him, and *He* would move Bill's heart if it were to be moved. If not, *He* would put the marriage to death according to His divine strategy and timetable. I would go home and love Bill, no matter what.

KNOWING GOD IN EXILE

But I would not go home alone. Like Moses at Mount Sinai, I cried out to God, "If your Presence does not go with [me], do not send [me] up from here" (Exodus 33:15). And I took His words to Moses as having been spoken to me: "My Presence will go with you, and I will give you rest" (33:14). In my going home to Bill, God would go with me, and in His coming with me and to me I would know myself deeply loved. More than that, because of God's presence with me, I knew I would not be destroyed, regardless of what Bill decided to do about our marriage.

Just before leaving the Biltmore Hotel, God's words recorded in Jeremiah 29, addressed to the Israelites living in exile in Babylon, offered me both comfort and challenge: "Build houses and settle down," God told His people living in that foreign land. "Increase in number there; do not decrease" (verses 5-6). *Settle down and plan to grow in your place of sorrow,* the Scripture seemed to say to me. *It may be a while.*

"Also, seek the peace and prosperity of the city to which I have carried you into exile," God said to His people, reminding them it was His own hand that had brought them to Babylon. "Pray to the LORD for it, because if it prospers, you too will prosper" (verse 7). *If you ask Me to bless Bill,* I felt God was saying, *you will benefit from that blessing, too.*

Then this promise: "'I know the plans I have for you,' declares the LORD, 'plans to prosper you and not to harm you, plans to give you hope and a future'" (verse 11). *I am a good God,* He was reminding me, *and My plans for you will validate your hope in Me.*

And finally this, "You will seek me and find me when you seek me with all your heart" (verse 13). *When you need Me more than life,* God assured me through His Word, *you will find rest in My presence.*

And I believed. I had no other choice. To whom else could I have turned? I knew I needed God more desperately than life.

My Biltmore experience was a dying, a recognition that I could no longer live one more day in my own strength. It is always at this point that God is gracious to show Himself. In our desperation we can see Him for who He is—the destroyer of our idols and the Savior we need. In Him is not only life but resources beyond our own to love others out of the overflow of His love for us.

When I came to God's table of tenderness and took nourishment from His love, I became able to go home and invite Bill with less demandingness to taste my redeemed heart, a kind of hors d'oeuvre of womanly kindness to whet his appetite for the Father's banquet of grace.

TWO GREAT AND TERRIBLE GIFTS

It took some time for Bill to believe that something had shifted in me that had enabled me to relinquish my demand (though not my request) for his kindness. As I came to rest more and more in the care of a good Father who cherished me as His precious daughter, my own heart was gradually changed. My compulsion to control Bill was more and more replaced by a compassionate love for him I'd not experienced before and could not myself have generated. God's love flowing into me flowed through me to Bill in the feminine voice. I had laid down my weapons against him; there was no way I could convince him to change. It was now Bill's turn to do battle with God. I had withdrawn from the fight, willing to wait for Bill to decide what to do about his life, his drinking, his relationship with God, his future with me.

Things got worse. But there came a weekend when Bill and I had a terrible fight and he stormed back to our bedroom where I was sure he was packing to leave. Instead, he came back to where I was crying and admitted he needed help. He didn't *want* to keep hurting me time and again, but he couldn't stop on his own. When I told him I couldn't help him, he said, "I know. I'll find someone who can." And he did.

Bill's words were welcome evidence of his longing to protect and cherish me. His willingness to seek help was a first step in bending his knee to the God with whom he was doing inner battle. But there were no sudden changes, no quick fixes, no dealing with the reality of his alcohol addiction. Just baby steps away from divorce and toward restoring our relationship. How can I tell of the years that followed—my often wild fluctuations between hope and despair, my inner battles to refrain from forcing Bill's hand or God's, the tantalizing tastes I had of husbandly kindness, the merciful coming of God's heart to mine, the sometimes interminable dailiness of my homemaking and writing and grappling with our son's adolescence? Two-and-a-half years of marital struggle after Bill first sought counseling had to pass before he acknowledged his alcoholism at a men's retreat and began to do serious business with God. And even that, of course, did not "fix" things, though his sobriety has opened the door to a far more authentic relationship than we've ever known before.

But *authentic* is far from *trouble-free*. If anything, our deeper level of honesty has plunged us more desperately than ever into a dependence on God. We never knew we needed Him that way in our days of denial and superficial connectedness. Relationships are intrinsically mysterious and unfailingly messy in a fallen world. This always flies in the face of our feminine compulsion to control. What Bill and I are learning is not how to better manage our marriage but how to more willingly repent of our love failures, how to more unashamedly beg God for His Presence, and how to more fervently worship when He comes.

As women we have been given two great and terrible gifts. One is to see not only our own fallenness, but also the fallenness of our men. We can see most clearly the sins of the ones we love most dearly: their fear and (what is worse) their moments of giving in to the fear; their running from what they should be running toward; their losses of courage and hope; their preoccupation with what they can control and their reluctance to enter what they cannot fully manage; their love of things because they fear they cannot bring competence to loving people well; their flight from God because they've known so little of submitting to and being loved by fathers who love them, much less a heavenly Father who loves them.

This we can see as women if we have the courage to face the truth; if we refuse to run from our disappointment; if we choose to believe our sadness will not destroy us. The truth is, our sorrow is not fatal, though it does indeed *feel* like death. The sorrow that comes when we receive this first of our two terrible gifts—seeing clearly both our own sinfulness and the particular fallenness of our men—opens us to receive the second terrible gift, the gift of loving them in spite of their sin.

Make no mistake: It is a gift, God's gift to us. It lies not within our power to love from our own resources. If men have done us harm, we cannot in our own strength do good to them.

But God can and does; He loves unto death those who have violated His law and wounded His heart by their idolatry. And because of Calvary and because of Pentecost, God's Spirit appropriates forgiveness to our spirits, and His grace toward us becomes ours to give. Now we as women can look at our men's sin and not compensate, minimize, sanitize, pretend, fix, or change any of it. We can simply see it and plead with God for His enabling to love them anyway.

That is the gospel, delivered to us and through us. Once I stopped running from the brokenness of my pain, I could be nourished by God, sacrifice my own agenda of forcing Bill to nourish me, and offer him the grace God had offered me. God can do the same thing in any life yielded to Him, and the hope He brings when He visits with His presence is a hope that "does not disappoint us" (Romans 5:5).

Will God change our circumstances? Maybe, maybe not.

Will He change our hearts? Without question. Will He bring us joy? More and more and more.

———————

Recognizing that every relationship is a mystery
to be entered rather than a problem to be solved,
may we approach both the Presence
and all our other connections more intent
on wonder than on mastery, more desirous of delight
than of decorum, and more concerned with
authenticity than with etiquette, to the praise
of our wondrously relational God.

———————

QUESTIONS FOR REFLECTION AND DISCUSSION
As we enter both the relinquishment of our control over others and the embracing of our sure hope in God, let us face with integrity the following questions.

1. When you've realized you can no longer control men, what experience have you had that God is enough to sustain your life?
2. In whatever relationship you presently find unfruitful, what are you saying to God about it?
3. What do you sense God saying in response?
4. How have you shown yourself willing to stay out of the battles God calls the men in your life to fight with Him?
5. What might it look like to relinquish your demand that men struggle with the same things and in the same ways you struggle with God?
6. How has God offered you hope even in the midst of a painful or difficult situation?
7. What can you legitimately hope for from God in those situations?
8. What are you doing to confront men's sin with bold love for their sakes?
9. What promises has God given you regarding your relationships with men?

PART THREE

Living as God's Daughters

CHAPTER SEVEN

OUR RESPONSE TO GOD'S IMAGE: RESPECTING MEN

*My husband needs to know that I respect him,
that I admire and trust him as a man.
And I do.*
CYNTHIA HEALD

My friend and I were enjoying an afternoon cup of tea while a winter storm blew outside, when her eyes clouded over with sudden sadness as she told me this story.

"The other night my husband and I went out for dinner with several other couples," she recalled. "Some of the men started picking at him. They were old friends, and their comments were mostly teasing. But each time they said something negative about him, I jumped in to defend him.

"Later that night," she went on, her voice dropping, "one of those friends drew me aside and said to me, 'You know, every time you step in to protect your husband, you emasculate him.'

"Well, that cut me to the quick," she admitted to me. "Never have words more powerfully true been spoken to me. I don't really want the job of protecting my husband, especially now that I've seen how disrespectful it's been for me to take care of him in that way."

I nodded my understanding, and we sat quietly a few

moments, contemplating the unintended harm we sometimes do in failing to respect our men.

HONORING MEN
When the Apostle Paul described how Christian husbands
and wives were to live out the new life of the Holy Spirit in
them, he gave separate instructions to husbands and wives
(Ephesians 5:22-33). His words to husbands (verses 25-30)
give voice to what our feminine hearts most want from men
as they move toward us with Christ's energy. We long to
receive their sacrificial love, their glad provision, their
unselfish protection, and their hearts' kind cherishing. In
these words not only does Paul call husbands to Christ-like
love, he also invites us as wives to embrace our longings
regarding our husbands. There is great hope for those of us
who are covenantally bound to redeemed men, for they are
indwelt by God's Holy Spirit, who is eager to recreate and
make more clear Christ's love for us through them.

On the other hand, Paul does not neglect to show us our
own obligations toward our husbands: "Wives," he says, "submit to your husbands as to the Lord" (5:22). And these
words, too: "The wife must respect her husband" (5:33). We
are to respond to men's sacrificial love with our trust and
respect, inviting them to be the husbands Paul instructs
them to be.

If men were perfect, our submission to and rest in their
leadership would pose predicament enough. After all, it's a
struggle for men and women to submit to *Christ's* perfect
leadership. But because of the fallenness of our human
nature, not only do we often fail to trust and respect our
husbands, they often fail us by retreating from instead of ini-
tiating love toward us. Thus we face the dilemma of longing
for men's love as described in Ephesians 5, while sometimes
experiencing the woundedness of their not coming to us or
not staying with us. How difficult it often is to follow the
leadership of imperfect men in a way that is both honest and
respectful.

CHOICES OF FAITH

Trust God and love men by respecting them. That is our task as redeemed women called to live out the two great commandments of Scripture in a world where disappointment in relationships is inevitable. To obey will demand a far greater faith than we are used to experiencing. It will require more than a theoretical trust in God. It will call for even more than a theological trust in Him. What we will need is a personal, relational trust in God that will sustain us in our struggle to comprehend and live out a life of genuine respect toward our husbands. We must come to know God in a way that is deep and solid enough to keep us from giving up in disgust or caving in to pretense. If we hope to live with integrity regarding what is in our hearts toward men, what must change in us is not an improved capacity to manage our longings, but a more passionate dependence on God as the only Source of our lives.

It will not always be easy. Faith often invites us to risk, and the risks we will or will not take reveal something about our faith. We live out what we most deeply believe about God in the day-by-day choices we make, especially regarding our relationships. Our faith in God is incarnate today and next week and next year; people watching us *know* whether we trust Him or not.

We cannot force ourselves to have faith in God, but when we act, we give evidence to the faith we do or do not have. The Canaanite prostitute Rahab, for example, was commended for her faith (James 2:25), not just because she believed the Israelite spies when they said they would show kindness to her and her family, but because she hid them from their enemies on the roof of her Jericho inn (Joshua 2). This was her faith revealed. She had no guarantee they would protect her—nothing except their word and what she saw in their eyes and what she knew of their God.

Given Rahab's profession as innkeeper/prostitute, it must have felt like a monumental risk to her to trust those men. It is likely that very few men had ever moved toward her with *her* well-being in mind. The gods with whom she was familiar were rapacious, bloodthirsty, and utterly capricious. How did she come to believe she could rest in the goodness of her enemy's God? Surely it was of faith, "and this not from [herself], it [was] the gift of God" (Ephesians 2:8). Rahab came to believe and to act on her belief by receiving God's gift of faith and trusting Him to keep her from being destroyed.

If we will depend on God for our very lives, we will find the courage to ask much of men in ways that will honor and delight them. When we trust the One who judges justly, we can risk respecting men by being open to them. We can live present to our feelings about them, sorrowing when they fail us and dancing when they give us tastes of their goodness, for we know our hearts are safe with God no matter how our men are behaving toward us. More than that, we can call forth and celebrate men's redeemed hearts as we see and respond to God's Spirit moving in them. The authentic giving of our hearts is one important way we obey Paul's instruction to respect our husbands.

RESPECT LIVED OUT

For many years I wrongly believed I was respecting Bill by hiding from him what was going on in my heart. I pretended I was unafraid of his alcohol abuse, unconcerned about his failure to protect me, and unaffected by his unkindness. I would not enter my Ephesians 5 longing for his provision, protection, and cherishing, because I did not believe he was capable of bringing those things to me. I was wrong—not only wrong to believe he *couldn't* provide, protect, and cherish me, but wrong to think I shouldn't ask him to do so.

Respect is a much misunderstood concept when it comes to the dynamics of male-female relationships. How men treat women (in word, deed, and attitude) and how women likewise treat men flows out of what they believe about each other. When we as women hold back our true feelings from men, there is always a reason for our pretense that exposes what we most fundamentally think of them. Perhaps we fear what they would do to us if they knew what we were thinking. I have known many women, for example, held hostage by their husbands' anger. Maybe we are too unsure of their love to risk opening our hearts to them. Too many women don't expect men to be good men, so it would be futile to protest their masculine unkindness. We disrespect men if we pretend we aren't affected when they hurt us, even when we recognize that the damage they do may be born out of their own fears and inadequacies.

There are *respect* issues that lie at the root of all our choices about what to say or do in our interactions with men. If, for example, we are convinced they are too fragile to bear the candor of our words, too insecure to stand up to our attempts at self-sufficiency, too intimidated by our chaos to speak kindly to calm it, or too relationally incompetent to know how to lead our families or wisely discipline our children, our belief will play itself out in the words we speak or refuse to speak, and in the things we do or choose not to do. What is in our hearts always leaks out for good or bad, to bless or damage, to offer compassion or condescension.

And our choices always have an impact on men. When we protect them instead of expecting them to protect us, when we treat them as emotional cripples by telling them how to handle their relationships, when we call them incompetent or bad-hearted, it reinforces their own sense of inadequacy regarding their ability to behave as good men. It may also cause them to turn their hearts away from us in shame and anger, and we will have sabotaged what we desire to give and they desire to receive: our heartfelt respect. More than that, as our children grow into adulthood, our sons will come to believe about themselves what we believe about men, and our daughters will expect all men to be as we have portrayed them. Both our sons and our daughters will be affected by our perceptions regarding men as they interact with the opposite sex, particularly when it comes to choosing a marriage partner.

We have too little understanding of how great our responsibility is to honor the men in our lives by believing in and calling forth the best in them. Particularly in our relationships with Christian men, our challenge is to believe that, because of the Holy Spirit living in them, they can model to us Christ's own character and gentle confidence. They as God's representatives can bring us His eyes of delight through their eyes, His words of love and direction through their own masculine voices. This we want them to do, but unless we believe this is also what they themselves most deeply want to do and *can* do because of their redemption, we will go on asking little or nothing of them, and in doing so will fail to respect them as we should.

If men are God's ambassadors to bring us the sacrificial love for which we yearn, we in turn are His ambassadors to bring men the honor and esteem they long to enjoy. Honor is a fragile and precious gift we can offer the men in our lives. Far too often we women have refused to give it, either out of revenge for our hurt or out of ignorance that we have it to give. We long to receive it from others, and we *have* received it from God. He honors us by showing us the wounds our sins have caused Him at the same time He issues His invitation to grace. It is time we risked being His conduit of a similar respect to men.

In learning to love men—especially redeemed men—with our genuine respect, two things are required of us as women of integrity: We must learn to wear white and we must call forth men's good hearts.

WEARING WHITE

If men retreat instead of move toward us with tender strength, we do not do them honor by ignoring their unkind or ungodly behavior. When men sin against us they sin against God who has called them to love us, and they distort the image of God in them. God doesn't pretend their sin makes no difference. What makes us think it's respectful to act as though *we* don't mind?

Our usual response to men's sin, however, is to try to control their behavior by shaming them or by speaking words to convince them how wrong they are, or by instructing them in how they *ought* to act. Generally, this approach disrespects men by moving the initiative for their behavior away from them and into our own hands. Because God honors our right to make choices about what we believe and how we act, we honor men by refusing to tell them what to do. Usually they already know what they should be doing. In any case, they are men, answerable to God regarding their actions. Our attempts to control them may, in fact, deflect their attention away from what God might want to say to them if He could be heard above our strident words.

Yet God also does not interfere forever with the consequences of what His children choose. Adam and Eve had to leave Eden when they ate the forbidden fruit. Hagar's pregnancy caused Sarai incredible pain. Moses' disobedience kept him from entering Canaan. The child born of David and Bathsheba's adultery died. The people of Israel were exiled to Assyria, the people of Judah sent to Babylon. We are not God's puppets, but neither do we escape His just judgment sooner or later. What we sow we reap. This is rich evidence of God's respect for us as His image-bearers, held accountable for making our own choices.

The question is, Who is responsible for executing God's judgment against men's sins? "It is mine to avenge," declares the Lord (Deuteronomy 32:35). But we women sometimes take it upon ourselves to rain down on men the just deserts of their misdeeds. We wrest judgment from God's hands and bring on men the consequences of their sin. We make them pay for their wrongdoing by our harsh words or our martyred silences or our calculated acts of retribution. In this we dishonor both God by usurping His role as Judge and men by heaping shame on their heads. There is a better way.

We give evidence of our respect for men not by *bringing* them the consequences of their sin, but by *showing* them the consequences of their sin as it affects us. We can show them our sadness when they let us down. When they do not bring us their hearts, we can let them know how lonely we are. At whatever point they do not protect us, we can tell them about our fear. When they do not treasure us or when they value the wrong things in us, we can offer them our tears of disappointment. In short, we can bleed when they wound our hearts—not to make them pay for their sin but to let them see what their sin has done.

Perhaps the most respectful thing we can do for men is to don a new emotional wardrobe, wearing white so that the blood drawn by their wounding of us shows most clearly. Instead of our words, we can sometimes offer them our eyes. There they will see our hurt and pain and fear. This is not the same as sulking or withdrawing, which is revenge. This is about sorrowing in men's presence when they do us harm, even as we continue to treat them kindly and remain willing to forgive them as often as they repent. We cry in front of them, but we refuse to close our hearts to them. We tell them how hurt or angry we are, then we prepare them their favorite meal. This is the hard work of the gospel God calls us to do, grieving as He grieves at our own sin, calling men to repentance and grace as He consistently does for us.

One woman put it this way: "When a husband hurts his wife, she must give him a picture of the gospel by weeping and then being kind, not in a condescending, manipulative way, but in a way that disturbs him. A husband will come to know more of God in a woman's tears and kindness than in her arguments or acts of vengeance."

Honoring and trusting men means we expect their goodness and are unwilling to ignore their unrestrained anger or verbal attacks or vindictive silence. We show we believe they can treat us kindly by standing unequivocally, even legally, against their physical abuse. Our failure to tell them we are hurt or afraid or repelled by their actions simply affirms what they already fear—that they are irredeemably bad men incapable of making godly choices.

If we believe in men's good intentions and in their *desire* to be good men (God looks on the heart and so should we), then our faith in them will be evident in our surprise and sorrow when they fail us. *I know this is not the real you,* our astonished sadness says. *What will you do about the blood on my white dress you just drew with your harshness?* If their hearts are indwelt by Christ's Spirit, we are right to ask them to live out of the best parts of those hearts. Wearing white is not just respectful, it is redemptive.

AFFIRMING MEN'S GOOD HEARTS

But if the truth be known, we are in far greater danger of missing men's good hearts than of missing their sinful hearts. We may deny our disappointment and anger, or we may refuse to deal with men regarding their sin against us because we do not want to rock our relational boats. But even if we won't deal honestly with them, we will either play the martyr and harbor our grudges or we will voice our anger and criticism about them to other people, especially our female friends.

What we are less convinced of is the goodness of a man's redeemed heart. When a man acts out of his good heart, we sometimes think it's not enough or not good enough or not soon enough. What is worse, we may not even recognize that a particular word or action has emerged from the Holy Spirit's movement in him. Certainly every heart is by nature tainted with weakness and sin, but we must never forget to be grateful for whatever evidence we see of the fruit of God's Spirit flowing from men's redeemed hearts. We can all take our cue from Mary Farrar, who said regarding her husband, Steve: "Even when a man isn't pleased with what he sees in his own heart, if he will share it with his wife, she can love him for his openness. When Steve admits how weak he sometimes feels, I admire his honesty tremendously." Especially when a man repents, we must offer our forgiveness openhandedly. Would that we all responded more like my friend

Karen Lee-Thorp who exclaimed, "When I see the signs of repentance in a man, I think, *Boy, is that ever attractive!*"

Far too often I fail to recognize what Bill says or does that reveals his redeemed heart toward me or others. I struggle to rest in his covering when he offers it, even though I have seen rich evidence that he is God's man. Bill cherishes me, yet I sometimes fail to enjoy and revel in it. He shows me his good heart, and I don't always acknowledge or affirm it. He offers me his wise perception, and I'm likely to trust my own or someone else's more.

Of course, my reluctance to trust Bill is ultimately a reflection of my struggle to trust the God who gave me this man as my head and covering. If God could direct Sarah's life through Abraham, He can lead me through the wisdom and instincts of my redeemed though fallen husband. God is not limited by the limitations of the men in our lives. If we will trust His goodness and His sovereign power, we can learn to trust the hearts of men as well.

How then do we trust God and love men with integrity, submitting to our husbands and showing respect for men? First, as described earlier, we must wear white emotionally, letting men see the damage their love failure has done to us. Our dismay and sadness are the proper responses to their sin. Second, we must affirm whatever we see that shows us they are redeemed men, believing in the nobility of their Spirit-directed hearts. We must offer them a vision of who they are, reaffirming their identity as God's sons and highlighting for them the good they have done. It blesses Bill when I remember and remind him that he is a wonderful man, naming some area of growth or kindness I see and appreciate in him. There is much to admire in him, and I delight to tell him about it.

Whenever we find evidence of men's good hearts, we must store it in our memory banks and bring it out whenever they act like they are not good men—not condescendingly, as toward little boys, but with genuine surprise, as befits a fellow image-bearer. *Don't lie to me and act as though you don't have a good heart,* we must insist with something akin to astonishment in our voice. *I know your heart—why are you not living like the good man I know you to be?* We must do with men's goodness what we have become experts at doing with their shortcomings—use it on them to show them who we most deeply believe them to be.

And finally, we must be open to confessing and repenting our own failure to respect them by not having grieved at their sin or danced at their goodness. Respect is elusive and there are no rules to follow. But the Holy Spirit is present to our redeemed hearts as well as to the hearts of redeemed men, and He is relentless to show us our love failures for the purpose of ushering us into repentance and grace every time we fail. This, too, is the gospel.

A WOMAN OF INTEGRITY
There is a woman whose story is told in 1 Samuel 25 who struggled with respecting both a man who would not repent, as well as a man who would. Her name is Abigail, and she lived during the time of Israel's history when King Saul was pursuing David to take his life.

Abigail, described as "an intelligent and beautiful woman," was married to Nabal, a wealthy Israelite from the tribe of Judah who "was surly and mean in his dealings" (verse 3). David, anointed as Israel's future king but hiding from Saul in the desert near Nabal's home, had protected Nabal's shepherds from marauding desert tribes without asking him for any payment.

However, at the time of sheep-shearing, David sent servants to greet Nabal and request that they be allowed to share in the food and festivities because of their earlier kindness. Nabal's reply showed his surly disdain not only for David's good heart but for God's promise to give David the kingdom. "Who is this David?" Nabal asked contemptuously. "Why should I take my bread and water, and the meat I have slaughtered for my shearers, and give it to men coming from who knows where?" (verses 10-11).

When David's men reported to him what Nabal had said, his response was swift: "Put on your swords!" he commanded (verse 13). Four hundred strong, they headed for Nabal's party.

Knowing that Nabal's response to David's servants had put their lives in jeopardy, Nabal's servants went to Abigail for help, saying, "Now think it over and see what you can do, because disaster is hanging over our master and his whole household. He is such a wicked man that no one can talk to him" (verse 17).

What should Abigail have done? How could she show respect to this wicked man who had endangered the lives of his entire household by his foolishness? She could have pretended he was a good man. She could have exposed his sin and tried her own devices for changing his mind. She could have simply prayed that God would spare his life and the lives of his servants. How does a woman give evidence of her faith in God in the midst of such a scenario?

There are no right answers. Sometimes God calls a woman to wait on His own movement to intervene on her behalf—this is what Sarai did in Egypt. At other times He calls her to challenge men whose faith is weak—Deborah gave such words to Barak when he refused to call up Israel's fighting men unless she came along (see Judges 4:8-10). But Abigail gave evidence of her faith in God in a different way.

First, she made arrangements to repay David for his earlier kindness, taking supplies of food and wine to intercept David and his armed men. Falling at David's feet, she then offered her gifts and appealed to David in a way that is an example to us as women: She named and called forth his good heart, reminding him of who he was—God's chosen and safe-kept heir to the throne. "Please forgive your servant's offense, for the LORD will certainly make a lasting dynasty for my master, because he fights the LORD's battles," she pleaded, affirming David's coming reign. "Let no wrongdoing be found in you as long as you live," she begged. "When the LORD has done for my master every good thing he promised concerning him and has appointed him leader over Israel, my master will not have on his conscience the staggering burden of needless bloodshed or of having avenged himself," she declared, expressing confidence that David would do what was right, for God's sake, and for the sake of his future usefulness as God's anointed king (verses 28-31).

Abigail appealed to the good parts of David's heart, refusing to believe that his homicidal intent accurately defined who he most deeply was. *You're a better man than this,* she was saying. *I expect that later you'll be glad you acted on the basis of who God says you are, not on your momentary anger toward a foolish man.*

It is no wonder David exclaimed to Abigail, "Praise be to the LORD, the God of Israel, who has sent you today to meet me. May you be blessed for your good judgment and for keeping me from bloodshed this day and from avenging myself with my own hands" (verses 32-33). David repented of his self-avenging plans, neither justifying what he had intended to do nor shaming Abigail for showing him how wicked it would have been for him to carry out those plans. More than that, David declared that it was God who had brought Abigail at just the right time and had kept him from killing her in his rage. Thus her own hope in God was vindicated as well as David's.

Abigail stood against David's sin not by whining or nagging or rebuking, but by affirming who God is and what He had promised to do for David. She also reminded David of who he was, expecting him to act on the redeemed parts of his heart rather than on the self-sufficiency that threatened to undo him. Instead of telling David what a bad man he was because of his intended vengeance, Abigail told him what a good man he was and urged him to act accordingly.

In this she acted most respectfully toward him. And he acted like the good man he was, saying to her, "Go home in peace. I have heard your words and granted your request" (verse 35). He not only repented; he blessed her as well.

Then Abigail went home and treated her husband with

a similar respect. "When Abigail went to Nabal, he was in the house holding a banquet like that of a king. He was in high spirits and very drunk. So she told him nothing until daybreak" (verse 36). Instead of shaming her husband in front of his guests and possibly inviting his inebriated anger on her own head (which would have shamed him later), Abigail waited until the next day when he was sober to tell him everything she had done to save his life and the lives of their servants.

Then "his heart failed him and he became like a stone" (verse 37). Abigail had offered Nabal the same opportunity she had offered David—to reveal what was in his heart regarding both his sin and his truest intentions. But Nabal, instead of showing he was a child of God's covenant by apologizing to his wife and to his servants and to David, confirmed what was most deeply in his heart: He was terrified at the thought of his close brush with death, but he remained unrepentant about his sin.

COURAGEOUS LOVE

How could Abigail have acted with such courage and integrity toward both of these men, one wicked and the other willing to repent? Something in her character allowed her to be both shrewd and kind in her relationships with her husband and with her future king. She somehow had the wisdom to recognize that she could stand in David's way because he was a good man, but that she was prudent *not* to stand in Nabal's way because he was a foolish and wicked man.

We know nothing about Abigail prior to this event described in 1 Samuel 25. But because she had lived with a man who was surly and mean in his dealings, a man given to drinking and swaggering, she could easily have been driven to either bitterness or self-pity about her life. She could have turned her energy toward controlling him or staying out of his way altogether. But we find neither self-pity, passivity, manipulation, nor bitterness in Abigail's words or actions. The respect with which she acted toward both David and

Nabal flowed rather from her belief in God. She was sure God would do what He had said about making David king; her plea to David was not just to preserve his own reputation, but to remember what God was intent on doing in his life. More than that, Abigail was willing to risk the wrath of Nabal by telling him (when he was sober) what she had done without his permission. In that way she was also trusting God with her own life and future.

And God did not remain silent. "About ten days later, the LORD struck Nabal and he died" (verse 38). God Himself brought Nabal's unrepented sin down on his head, avenging the good heart of his servant David. And after Nabal's death, David sent for Abigail and asked her to become his wife. And she did.

The attitude or mood that surrounds a woman as she relates to men says much about her heart. The woman whose heart is not hardened toward men can come to them with kindness and deep respect. She may not like where they are on their journey, but she can relinquish her condescending or critical spirit, choosing instead to speak both graciously and wisely.

As women we always undo men when we submit to their need for a companion who will be present to what is going on in their hearts and behavior—not pretending about their depravity, but always responding in the context of their nobility. We must be present to both sadness regarding the evidence we see of their weakness and to longing and gratitude regarding the evidence we see of their dignity. In the process we must become willing to live in the "here" and the "not yet," trusting in the only One worthy of our unfeigned hope.

As we increasingly rest our hearts in God's heart, we will begin changing the way we see ourselves and the men in our lives. The change may be sudden or gradual, but our hearts will soften into kindness, even toward those who sometimes do us harm. We will become windows through which God's love will shine into the lives of others. Because He has smiled and kissed our once-raging heads, we can bless any who will abandon their own anger and receive our tenderness and blessing. Particularly with men, we can then become not just more honest but more compassionate. In this we will show forth the very face of God.

———————

Out of the realization that men's hearts
are both tainted by sin and yet able to image
God's own heart when redeemed by His grace,
let us reflect what God is like
as we sorrow when men sin against us
and celebrate when they pursue God
and us with holy passion.

———————

QUESTIONS FOR REFLECTION AND DISCUSSION
The desire we have that men would bring us their hearts, committed to our well-being and delighted with who we are, requires that we receive those masculine hearts with openness. We should not pretend they are better than they are, but neither should we fail to affirm what God has done and continues to do in them, particularly as His redeemed image-bearers. Within that context, pose these questions to your own heart.

1. How have you experienced men retreating from you?
2. In what ways have your responses to that retreat been respectful of them?
3. If someone were to watch you for one week, what would they name as your deepest beliefs about men from listening to your words and watching what you do to and for men?
4. What have your sons and daughters learned about what men are like from what you say or do?
5. How have you wronged men by bringing them the consequences of their sin (paying them back), rather than by showing them the consequences of their sin (being sad or afraid or disrupted)?
6. What evidence do you have that the men in your life have been redeemed?
7. How are you affirming the good things men do for you or others?
8. In what specific ways have you honored the men in your life?
9. In what ways will you commit yourself to honoring men in the future?

CHAPTER EIGHT

OUR HABIT OF WAIT: INVITING MEN'S MOVEMENT

Waiting and inviting are feminine things.
KAREN LEE-THORP

*J*an Frank and I were deep in conversation about how God kept bringing us back to lessons we thought we'd already learned, when suddenly she jumped up and said, "Hold on! Let me show you the illustration I use in my teaching to demonstrate what our Christian walk is like."

She brought out a circular copper tube that flattened neatly around itself, like a coiled rope. Then she pulled on each end of the tube so it stretched into a spiral.

"I believe we're wrong to think our Christian walk is like climbing a ladder, always moving upward" Jan said. "To me, it's more like circling along this spiral. We may come around to struggle with a particular issue time and again, but we're always going forward, continually being conformed to Christ's image as we move along our cyclical path of faith."

Jan's copper coil was a picture of God's kind relentlessness in bringing us again and again into a clearer reflection of His character in us. Sanctification is not a destination, it's a journey. We hate it that patterns take a long time to change, but what Pat Palau said to me is true: "Bad habits develop slowly, slowly, slowly, and they will have to be back-tracked piece by piece." The process takes a lifetime, but God will honor His own purposes and He seldom speeds things up.

RELATIONAL SANCTIFICATION
We, too, must respect the lifelong process of personal spiritual growth both in ourselves and in others. On the one hand, we are wrong to disdain the journey we have traveled with God. The roads we walk with God are never wasted; even our detours fit into His plan to conform us to Christ's image and to give witness to His grace. God's timing is never a mistake; when we're ready, He shows us the next step, but we cannot hasten our readiness.

On the other hand, we are equally wrong not to discern and affirm what God has done and is doing in the lives of others, especially men. Their detours, too, have their reasons, and we cannot fast-forward their spiritual progress. Because men's walk with God is often unlike our own, it's easy to dismiss their spirituality as inferior to ours. But we must learn to see with the eyes of faith the work God is doing (however slowly or subtly) in both their hearts and ours.

Our Christian life is the story of our relationship with a personal God, and relationships cannot be programmed. They are mystifying, gratifying, puzzling, and frustrating— sometimes all at the same time. We don't *do* relationships; we *live* in them. Who we are in them continually changes. That is both the beauty and the perplexity of worshiping a personal, relational God.

God describes Himself in terms of His relationships within Himself and with us. He also intends to reveal and express Himself through *our* relationships with each other. Men show us God's face of kindness and delight when they love and cherish us, and our responsiveness to them reflects God's own love within the Trinity. Our sanctification is intended to give evidence of the goodness of the God who indwells us, showcasing the glory of His steady love for us and through us.

Because our relational sanctification is essentially God's revelation of His redeeming love in us through His Holy Spirit, we do not govern sanctification—neither our own nor our men's. Like the wisest of parents, our Father-God knows what needs changing in our relationships, and we can rest assured He will address those things at just the right time and in the best possible way.

Though we cannot control our sanctification, we can (and often do) impede it. When the Holy Spirit nudges us to repent and change, we can choose whether to obey or resist. Yet even in that choosing we show forth the goodness of the God who woos us without coercion.

As we grow in grace, we must learn to wait, for we can neither force nor rush our own relationship with God. Nor can we as women push or hurry men to respond to God's overtures of love or our own invitations to greater intimacy. Sanctification cannot be hastened; waiting is essential.

WAITING AS RESPONDERS

Our waiting and inviting of men requires utter dependence on God. It also requires the sacrifice of our deeply ingrained self-centeredness as we cooperate with God's sanctifying work in us. As we women follow God's call to enter renewed relationships with men, several qualities will characterize our process of relational sanctification—not all at once, but in spiraling increments.

For one thing, we will increasingly live as responders rather than initiators in our relationships with men. Once while attending a networking meeting for Florida ministry leaders, I rose from my chair and went to greet a friend I saw in an adjoining room. When I reached him he gently chided, "You didn't have to come to me; I would have come to you." His kind but humbling words addressed my fear that I would go unnoticed if I did not initiate. We often doubt that men will move toward us unless we scramble to connect with them.

But quietness of spirit is God's work within our hearts, transforming us to practice the hardest but perhaps most quintessentially feminine thing we do, which is to wait. We may not like it, but biology teaches us that we are wait-ers. Our femininity is confirmed monthly; we are bound by time in ways that men are not. We are also receivers, dependent on men to come to us. And when we bear children, we are forced to wait nine months for God to do His secret work in bringing our love union to full fruition.

More than that, we do not set the limit on our waiting; when the baby is ready to be born, we are compelled to *not* wait. We cannot say, "I think I'll have this baby next week— I'm a little busy today." When the baby is ready to be born, it is not according to the convenience of our schedules. Waiting (which also means we are not in control) is a distinctively feminine thing.

Sometimes we do not like it that we are receivers and responders rather than movers and initiators in our relationships with men. We like it even less that we are called to submit and wait, especially when our dismay is rooted in experiences with men who have misused their masculine initiation in some way.

Yet our call to be responders and wait-ers is God's kindness to us as His female image-bearers. Our waiting and responding reflect the relating that exists within the Trinity, where there is the perfect balance of initiation by the Father and submission by the Son, as well as utterly selfless responsiveness on the part of the Holy Spirit sent by both Father and Son. More than that, the Triune God waits to bring all of history to completion, the Father setting the time, the Son awaiting the signal, the Spirit groaning in anticipation and intercession for us. God both validates and models submissive responsiveness, not as a curse, but as a way of being in relationships that displays His own nature and character.

Our call to submission mirrors God's image as gloriously as men's call to selfless love.

And we must not forget that, because God created us for oneness in diversity, the mingling of initiation and submission in our relationships with men is not an either-or thing. Mary Kassian offered this interesting perspective: "Being made in God's image means that both men and women have initiation and responsiveness in their character, but with differing emphases for male and female. The male is primarily characterized by initiation, but for him to initiate properly, he needs a responsiveness in his spirit so he's tender and compassionate toward the needs of others. Otherwise he tends to be like a plow, going his way and running people over. Women, on the other hand, are primarily responsive creatures, but for them to respond properly, they need initiation in their lives to avoid being doormats or to keep from responding to wrong people or wrong philosophies." Thus it is not a question of either/or but of emphasis and balance as together we image God.

RESTRAINING OUR WORDS

Another aspect of our habit of wait is our willingness to restrain our words. Over the years we as women have perfected the craft of word-wielding, and something deep within us rebels when the Apostle Peter tells wives that their unsaved or spiritually deflated husbands "may be won over without words by the behavior of their wives" (1 Peter 3:1). Won *without words?* How can it be done? Why should it be done? What's wrong with words?

Nothing is wrong with words, of course. God spoke the universe into existence, and Jesus Himself is called the Word (John 1:1). Our human words and our physical eyes are the vehicles by which we convey what is in our hearts, for good or evil. What then is Peter's reason for urging us as women *not* to bring words to our men? How can he leave us with only our eyes as windows to our souls?

Perhaps we must face what is true about the usual function served by our words, acknowledging, for example, how often we use words to fill in the quiet spaces of our loneliness. I have known women who, if they were to stop speaking, would have no recourse but to burst into tears because their aloneness (especially in a disappointing marriage) is such a palpable reality. I often find I would rather talk than cry. A friend once wisely restrained me from talking with her until I'd taken some time to be alone and weep, because I was using my words to keep from entering my sorrow.

I have also known the usefulness of words to justify something I've said or done. Defensive sentences often spring unbidden to my mind and out of my mouth before I have time to check or modify them. Words also serve to prove my emotions are valid, especially when I am being shamed or criticized for feeling a certain way. And who has not appreciated the value of words to pay back others' unkindness with unkindnesses of our own?

Words have been our lawyers; how can we defend our case if we are to be without them? How cruel of Peter to point to Jesus as our example, saying that "[when] they hurled their insults at him, he did not retaliate; when he suffered, he made no threats. Instead, he entrusted himself to him who judges justly" (1 Peter 2:23). This is a hard saying.

And what of my wielding of words to convince others of the wisdom of my way of seeing and doing? God has given me insight about many things, and I sometimes see truth my husband cannot see or has not seen, It seems natural to use words to prove I'm right about something. In fact, I must admit I find it puzzling that Jesus didn't bring more words to the rich young ruler who walked away from Him (Matthew 19:16-22). The perfect Word-giver surely had more He could have said. I would have said more.

And therein lies the clue to our being told to win men without words. It is the illicit use to which we sometimes put our words that exposes the importance of our restraining them. When we use words to avoid our sorrow, to protect ourselves, to avenge our mistreatment, or to control others' behavior, our words run contrary to God's design for us. When we embrace silence in lieu of a proliferation of words, God has opportunity to both move on our behalf and carry out His plan for others without the interference of our verbal agendas.

We exercise our habit of wait by giving up our attempts to use words to manipulate men into doing what we want. It may be as minor as the incident one woman described as "an anguished conversation" she had with her husband one midnight regarding an unresolved relational problem. "I can't go to sleep until I know we're right on this and together again," she had pleaded, to which he had replied, "I'm too tired. Can't it wait until the morning?" We hate to wait even eight hours to do what we feel needs to be done, particularly when it comes to resolving conflict in the significant relationships in our lives. We demand immediate relief, but men usually process relational matters through reflection. I want to move and fix things right now, but when Bill says, "Let me think about it," I am learning to say, "Okay, I'll wait." As difficult as it is, we must give up our determination to make things happen and instead learn to live quietly with gracious poise and a maturity of silence, confident that God is at work even in the most impossible situation.

There's something out of control about waiting that we cannot countenance and find excruciatingly hard to do. In fact, waiting is all about giving up control—not in a capitulation of responsibility, but in a quietness of trust, even in our sorrow. We would rather move than mourn, rather stay busy than weep, rather be finished than wait for God. We're generally convinced that we know best and that our way is the only right way. And in our refusal to be God's ladies in waiting, we push others, especially men, to live according to our agendas and timetables.

Cinny Hicks described our feminine spirit of control in these words: "Women have a false belief they can actually make men change. But when men start feeling crowded by us, they will start retreating. And then we don't let them retreat. We keep following them into the next room, talking or nagging because we're not sure they're hearing what we are saying. We women don't know when to stop, but we're going to have to let them go."

To rest in someone else's judgment and timing—even God's—means we must lay down our watches and our whistles and our Day-Timers, and embrace a purpose higher than ourselves. This higher purpose has to do with living out our trust in God by submitting ourselves to *His* agenda—not ours or that of the men in our lives. Our individual stories are but a part of a much larger story and purpose, which is to showcase God's grace and thereby draw others to the only One who can enable us to do what is so clearly supernatural. God will gift us to bless out of our broken hearts because He wants to show Himself to others through what we say and do.

ACTIVE WAITING

Relinquishing control and learning to wait is rich evidence of the Holy Spirit's sanctifying work in the life of a godly woman. It marks her as a woman who trusts both in God's sovereignty and in His benevolent intentions for her life, particularly in her seasons of distress.

"*Wait* has been a key word in my life," Luci Shaw told me. "*Wait, wait, things aren't always going to be like this. Things will shift; don't make a move now. Wait and see God work.*

"It's hard for us as women to be still and know that God is God," Luci admitted. "But if we won't learn to wait, we'll become arrogant, thinking we can solve all our own problems. Waiting makes us vulnerable and willing to say, 'This is beyond me, God. Please move in to help me or lead my husband to do something here. I can't do it by myself.'"

God smiles at such prayers, and the angels throw a party at our repentance for having worshiped our self-sufficiency. When we embrace the reality that God gets to be God, we enjoy sweet tastes of rest that heighten our hunger for

Home, even as they settle our hearts to wait more resolutely for Him to come to us.

And while we wait for God to move, what are we to do? God does not call us to passivity, but to active waiting. We are to wait for men as the Church waits for Christ, her Bridegroom, longing for His coming, preparing for His arrival, purifying herself in anticipation of His face shining on her, and inviting Him in at every turn. She does not hesitate to ask for His initiation, His covering, His provision, His protection, and His cherishing. She grieves the necessity of waiting (*How long?* she cries out), but there is the eternal springing of hope in her heart as well.

And that is how we as women are to wait actively for good men. As God's ambassadors, we are called to "do what is right" (1 Peter 3:6). We are not required to say *no* words, but rather, out of the "purity and reverence" of our lives, to offer only words that edify. Paul offers these guidelines regarding our words: "Do not let any unwholesome talk come out of your mouths, but only what is helpful for building others up according to their needs, that it may benefit those who listen" (Ephesians 4:29).

We are called to discover ways to use our feminine words for building men up according to their needs so they will be benefited by listening to us. And that will require that we examine again the purpose of our words, for our motive and mood and method of speaking are as important to God as the words we say. What is a godly motive for the words we bring to men? In a word, *invitation*.

INVITING WITHOUT DEMANDING
When God uses words, His motive is always to invite His image-bearers to return to relationship with Him through repentance and faith. Even Jesus' strong words to the Pharisees regarding their hypocrisy culminated in His words of longing that they would be willing to be drawn to Him (Matthew 23).

It is crucial to remember that, before we can issue words

of invitation to men, we must first respond to God's invitation to bring our own hearts to Him—both with our words and with our silence. We are invited to speak freely to God, no holding back. We tell Him our sorrow and joy, our requests and our praise; we speak our anger, our trust, our confession, and our gratitude—He gets to hear it all.

Then—and this is crucial—after we have spoken to Him, we listen. God has much to tell us in our silence before Him, words from both His written Word and through His Holy Spirit's voice. Through them He conveys His tender comfort, His unabashed delight, His firm (but never harsh) rebuke, His clear directive—whatever it is we most need to hear. Our silence before Him is our opening of the door of our hearts so that He can enter, bringing supper with Him to sustain our souls (Revelation 3:20). If we will be still, He will come, and His coming will nourish us.

Mary, the mother of our Lord Jesus, is a good example for us. No woman in the Bible received more startling news than Mary when Gabriel announced to her that she, a virgin, would bear "the Son of the Most High" (Luke 1:32). It is evidence of her integrity that she did not reduce the mystery to words, but rather "treasured up all these things and pondered them in her heart" (Luke 2:19). Mary's pondering over God's movement in her life was reflective worship, an invitation to the Holy Spirit to do His unseen work of revealing to her what was in her heart through the events surrounding her life.

We women would do well to ponder more so that our words flow from our worship. So often we are quick to speak what is on our minds, especially to men, and the proliferation of our own words often moves us away from, instead of closer to, the words God wants to speak to us. Are we willing to listen to God's voice so that what we speak comes only from what He is whispering in our ear? Jesus told His disciples, "These words you hear are not my own; they belong to the Father who sent me" (John 14:24).

Leanne Payne has said: "There is a difference between

spiritualized perfectionism and our walk in the Spirit. So often we try to substitute conceptual knowledge about God for a day-by-day walk with Him. It causes an awful rift between the head and the heart. We must learn to know and stay in touch with our own hearts every day, kneeling before God and listening to Him, then moving to obey Him only and whenever He speaks."

Our words to men must always be gospel words, which often involves inviting men to repent of their sin. As we show men our broken hearts at their sin, we show them God's broken heart at their sin. Women who never say any words to men about how they are being treated may be dishonoring those men (and thereby disobeying God's Word through Peter) if their motive is to keep the peace or to make men pay for their sin by the silent withholding of their feminine hearts.

Of course, God desires that we choose what to say or not to say in a way that reveals our deepest belief that God is in control and we're not. Jan Frank spoke truly when she said, "A woman must speak the truth in love to her husband if he is not pursuing his calling with God. But she must also come to a point of surrender, where she can pray, *God, you know my heart's desire. I've spoken the truth in love, and now this man is in your hands.*"

We must remember that it is God who is the breaker and draw-er of men's hearts, not we. None of us chooses God of our own initiative; He comes wooing our hearts. Jesus said, "No one can come to me unless the Father who sent me draws him" (John 6:44), and it is evidence of our faith in the Father's work and timing when we wait for Him to draw the hearts of the men we love.

We, however, must stand ready to invite men to receive God's grace (and our own) when they do repent. Together we can then join in a dance of praise for God's goodness, showing forth the gospel to a sinful world. With our invitation words we can also ask men to be good men for us, as Abigail asked David. Men may not always know what it is that we desire from them: their kindness, their eyes of delight, their strength on our behalf, or their words of comfort. And so we must sometimes ask for what we need. Susan Yates said: "We women often expect men to guess how to meet our needs, but it's not fair to ask them to read our minds. They aren't God."

Sometimes what we must ask from men is simply their presence with us. Dale Hanson Bourke told me, "I once interviewed Kevin Leman, and he said what a man needs to do is sit in his wife's mud puddle with her and put his arm around her. She doesn't want him to pull her out of the mud puddle; she just wants him to come sit with her in the middle of it."

My husband, Bill, observed that men often approach women's mud puddles with a long stick for pulling them out without getting muddy themselves. Jesus, however, was not reluctant to get muddy by entering our mess. The mud/blood on His body reminds us He knows our frame and our pain, having become by His incarnation our "merciful and faithful high priest" (Hebrews 2:17). When we invite men to join us in our mud puddles without demanding that they fix what's wrong or make us feel better, men are free to model Christ to us in ways we deeply need and can receive, identifying themselves with us in our distress and comforting us with their words and presence.

Yet when we ask, we must do it without demanding that men provide what we want when and how we think best. We must not stamp our foot or tap our toes, but merely invite men to the dance of being good men for us.

We also must do our asking without being critical of what they have or have not done in the past. Kathy Peel rightly observed that "any time we try to shape our mates into something other than what they are or criticize them because they're not doing things the way we do them, we're putting ourselves up as the standard of what is right and expecting them to conform—and that's really self-idolatry."

Moreover, when men bring us what we have requested of them, we must not weigh their gifts in the balance of our expectations to see how they measure up. "If you want a man to do certain things," cautioned Pat Palau, "you'd better be satisfied with the way he does them, because criticism of the things he's trying to do is crushing." Another woman added this thought: "We've been praying all along for our husbands to change, but if their change does not come in the package we expect it to come in, we distrust them and continue to hold them at bay for a couple years." Sadly, this is often true.

WORDS OF BLESSING
Our invitation words can bring blessing to men's lives. Words of encouragement and kindness are as important to the hearts of men as their tender words are to our hearts. We are wrong to think we can make a man feel large by making him feel little with our words. We can't "beat him up" with our criticism of him or his character and then expect him to feel strong or act compassionately on our behalf. Even when we come with candid words, we must examine the motive and mood beneath them. "It's not bad for me to tell my husband how I feel," my friend Judy Vander Plate said, "but it depends on how I tell him. I've had to reevaluate how the words come out of my mouth." We all would do well to follow her example, asking ourselves, "Am I being kind, both in my choice of words and in my timing of them?"

We women need not say everything we think about any given subject in our conversations with men. Our tendency is to speak in paragraphs, even chapters, when all that's required is a sentence. Men don't need to know all the details. More than that, we women don't have to say all we know as soon as we know it. Sometimes, in fact, we must wait a long time to say what must be said, trusting that God will show us when the time is right.

Except when our waiting is motivated by fear (as is often the case, for example, when we are caught in abusive relationships), we are right to restrain ourselves from acting immediately on all we know. Jody Engel wisely remarked, "We think waiting is a mark of weakness or cowardice, but it takes great strength and courage to know something and not speak to it or act on it. God has infinite power, but consider the self-restraint with which He uses that power.

"We women have incredibly active minds, and we love to fix and control," she went on. "But for us to wait and not speak is a reflection of the heart of God, who knows what to do but chooses to wait until the timing is right. Waiting requires sacrifice. In women it involves groaning, and I think there is something very noble in it." Like the woman in labor who recognizes that she must restrain herself from pushing until it is in her baby's best interest, so we must sometimes groan as we wait, refusing to relieve our pain by trying to "fix" our men or by filling our emptiness with words.

God teaches us much through His own waiting to speak, modeling for us how to be shrewd with our words—not because the words we might bring aren't true, but because it would not be respectful to tell men what to do, or good timing to say all we know when we know it.

We also can offer men an invitation to trust our hearts. We do that when we give evidence through our words that we respect them. Pamela Reeve expressed the importance of respecting men when she recalled her interactions with young men over the many years of her teaching career. "A man fears having his weaknesses be discovered," Pamela declared. "He worries, *If I really let a woman know who I am, she won't want me. If I show my weakness, the one thing I want she'll never give. I'll be found inadequate and she'll lose all respect for me.*

"Unfortunately," Pamela added, "that is too often true. Women can easily sabotage men's masculinity by belittling them for their inadequacy or by usurping their leadership in the family."

When men show us who they are, our words and attitude of respect should be our invitation to them to trust our love and kindness toward them, even as their heavenly Father remembers their frailty and has compassion on them. My sister, Peg De Boer, said it so well: "A man wants to be able to trust that his wife won't make light of the risks he takes in expressing his vulnerability to her. Women can easily trample into a deeply personal area in a man's life and sort of overwhelm it. A man needs to know that when his wife has seen something nobody else has seen, she will treat it carefully and with great respect." This doesn't mean, of course, that we have to protect men or keep their boundaries for them. But we must revere the intimacies they share with us and no one else.

Barbara Feil repeated that theme in this story she told about an experience she had with her husband. "Not long ago," she said, "Bruce told me about something I'd done to hurt him, and for a moment I stepped outside myself and listened as my husband's friend. As his wife I was deeply threatened, but as his friend, I was honored he was sharing something deep and intimate, and I treated it as something sacred." Good words from a wise woman.

GRACE AND GRATITUDE

Perhaps the most important words we can speak to men are words offering our forgiveness when they show us their hearts of repentance. Forgiveness doesn't mean we won't feel hurt or angry when others sin against us. Nor is forgiveness a once-and-for-all event. Rather, it is a state we live in that reflects God's refusal to give up on us, even though He knows the details of our most hidden sins. We can learn to cultivate the same spirit of mercy toward others that God extends toward us when we repent.

If we live in God's forgiveness, we can have courage to face others' sin, because we know their sin against us is not fatal, and we don't have to leave. We can stay and grieve, accept and love, and humbly offer them grace. Jody Engel wisely said, "When a man repents, a woman can offer him the grace of forgiveness, and he will see there is something in her that enables her to love him even when he is unlovable. In grace there is intimacy. Grace knows something ugly about you, but it doesn't back off, and it doesn't love you any less."

No woman will be able to forgive a man, of course, unless she has been broken by her own sin, recognizing her need for grace even as she offers it to others. It is not easy for any of us to live needing grace as desperately as we all do. Something deeply self-protective in us moves us either to justify ourselves for the wrong we have done or to intensify our efforts never to be wrong so we never have to ask for grace. My friend Penny Freeman put it this way: "I'm learning to rest in God's presence as a sinner who needs grace and who can expect grace to come every time I need it. It's so much better than trying not to need grace or trying to store it up for when I sin—you know, like stockpiling manna. It's hard to stop scrambling to stay connected to God without being dependent on Him, but I'm enjoying my tastes of just being still and letting Him overwhelm me with who I am in His sight."

The willingness to need grace because we have sinned refers not only to our relationship with God, but to our relationships with men. When one woman said of her husband, "This man is a vehicle of grace in my life," I was struck by the contrast in my own life. So often I am reticent to ask Bill's forgiveness when I have wronged him. How much easier it is to be in the power position of offering him grace than to stand in the place of needing it from him.

Yet being broken by our sin against others as well as by our sorrow over others' sin against us is intrinsic to our relational sanctification as believers. Regarding our need for God's comforting grace in the face of others' sin against us, Mary Kassian said, "We can only deal with our heaped up disappointments by allowing God to give us extra grace so we can remain free from bitterness. Going to God, who is our loving Father, and crying on His lap is a release for the disappointment we feel. We can then receive the Father's love in order to extend forgiveness to others." These, indeed, are gospel words.

And regarding our need for God's forgiving grace

because of our own sin, Leanne Payne said, "When we've seen our own souls, we have to say, *If God could offer grace to me, He can offer it to anyone.*" This, too, is the gospel.

Finally, there is one other kind of invitation words we can offer men: our words of gratitude. When they initiate kindness, when they are faithful in their jobs, when they protect us from mistreatment, when they offer us their words and their eyes of love, we must not forget to be thankful. And we must be satisfied with what they bring.

"When a man gives of himself," one woman said, "he wants her to say 'Thank you,' and not, 'Could you do it this way?' So often when men give us gifts, we tell them they could have done better or we give them the feeling it wasn't what we wanted. Men long to give their hearts and have it be enough."

Cynthia Heald offered these wise words: "Often a woman will say to a man, 'You play the game by my rules, and then I will be happy.' But even when men play by the rules we set up, we're often discontent. We think, *If my husband will just become a Christian, it will be good.* Then, *If he would just enter this Bible study.* Then, *If he would be a Sunday school teacher.* That's just the way we are. We always seem to want more."

If, however, we women will speak grateful words to men, moving toward contentment instead of comparison, we will mirror God's own encouragement of "Well done, good and faithful servant." Our heavenly Father's desire is that we offer men His own commendation in the feminine voice, affirming how they bless our lives. Valerie Bell told me, "A couple years ago I felt God was saying to me, 'Tell your husband you appreciate him.' So I said to Steve the next morning, 'Thank you for going to work for me today. Because you're working like you are, I have this wonderful luxury of being able to write and develop myself.'

"I'll never forget the look on his face," Valerie said, smiling at the memory. "It was such a shock for him, but I could tell he really liked it."

Would that more of God's daughters shocked more of His sons in similar ways!

THE HABIT OF INTERCESSION

As we practice the habit of waiting and inviting the movement of good men toward our hearts, what will be required of us? Certainly we will come to realize the necessity of sustaining our own intimacy with the God who alone can guide our footsteps away from self-centeredness toward kindness in our relationships with men. We sustain that intimacy by developing a habit of prayer and putting down roots in His Word.

We also will need other women, especially mature Christian women, who will walk alongside us and offer perspective. A friend once made this observation: "The glory of an older woman is that she can teach her spiritual daughters how to long for the Lord and how to long for good men, and then how to respond to God and to good men when they come. A mature woman in the Lord can encourage the woman at the point of despair, who is broken by her longing and saying 'I will die unless God comes.' The mentor can say, 'Be courageous. Wait. The Lord will come to you. He may send you a good man to walk with you or He may not. But the Father will come and He will send the Comforter.' This is the legacy of a woman who herself has invited God in and then has waited for Him until He came."

As much as we need encouragement and guidance from our friends and mentors, our greatest need is for the prayers of God's people. "We should never underestimate the power of prayer," said Susan Yates. "God can do miracles if His people pray. We should pick one or two women who can keep confidences and who are for us and for our marriage, and ask them to bathe us and our families in prayer. Ultimately, we can't change anything. It must be the Lord who does it."

We must recognize we cannot control whether or not men will repent toward us or toward God. We can try to control men's actions, but we will be only marginally successful (if at all) and deeply disappointed if it works. If we are honest, men's changed behavior does not satisfy us unless their hearts are changed as well. When we bleed respectfully and ask for men's kindness, their hearts may be *exposed,* but then we must pray and wait on God for those hearts to be *changed.* "How much energy do we want to spend on trying to change someone else?" asked Dale Hanson Bourke. "Ultimately, only God can change them anyway."

Living without guarantees (the men we love may repent and come to us, or they may not) forces us to look finally to God in steadfast intercession. A wise woman once told me, "For some years now I've been laying my hands on my husband while he sleeps and praying for him, and I have seen him begin to receive God's blessing. I realized that the critical spirit I'd had toward him and my prayers against him had actually been holding him back. Nothing positive comes from criticism, but much good comes from praying blessing on him."

Especially when we are living in covenantal relationships that are disappointing or unsatisfying, we must seek the face of God without ceasing. Edith Schaeffer said, "This is the word I have for the woman who has been disappointed in her marriage: Maybe your husband will change. Pray day in and day out, but don't nag him. You have married him, and this is whom you promised to love, honor, and obey. Your responsibility is as a wife, so be as good a wife to him as you possibly can. And then pray more than ever before, especially when he is not in the house. Take a day of fasting and prayer. Pray for him. Pray for greater oneness between you. But pray that the Lord will give you grace sufficient to do what is being a good wife to him, because that is what you have promised to do." Challenging words, and true.

As redeemed women committed to responding to God's call to trust Him and love others, we are invited to rest in Him, looking to Him both for our lives and for the redemption and sanctification of the men we love. "Until by our chaste and respectful behavior we women quit nagging men and let them go and let God have them, nothing can happen," Holly Phillips said earnestly. "We must learn to honor God and respect our husbands and let God deal with them, looking at things from God's perspective and remembering that His timing is perfect. We're so afraid to give up control, because if we lose control, what will happen to us? Probably the most incredibly wonderful thing we could possibly imagine!"

And wouldn't that be just like God? Maybe not right away, and certainly with no guarantee that our circumstances will conform to our expectations, we can be sure that if we will give up control and trust in Him, we will become God's own handmaidens of rest, waiting for and inviting His advent to our hearts so we can wait for and invite the coming of men's hearts as well. And that will indeed be the most incredibly wonderful thing we could possibly imagine.

In the belief that God is good, even in the face of our sometimes deferred hope for our own spiritual maturing and the spiritual maturing in the men who occupy our lives, may we be encouraged by Paul's words to the Philippian Christians: "He who began a good work in you will carry it on to completion until the day of Christ Jesus" (1:6).

QUESTIONS FOR REFLECTION AND DISCUSSION
As we learn to bring our hearts to men and wait for their hearts in return, we must not forget that God is intimately involved in that process. Because His Spirit is ever ready to work in hearts devoted to Him, we can yield ourselves to His sovereignty and His timetable in our ongoing relational sanctification, even as we struggle to keep alive our longing for the hearts of men. As a tool along that journey, ponder these questions.

1. What is the greatest hindrance to your relational sanctification?
2. If *you* have been doing the pursuing in your relationships with men, what keeps you from waiting for their pursuit?
3. How can you model the Bride who waits for Christ?
4. Why is it so hard to wait and pray for men to change?
5. What is the difference between worshiping God when men repent and when they don't?
6. In what ways can you show respect to men even when you bring them words of candor?
7. How can you practice really listening to men?
8. What can you do if you think your husband doesn't deserve your respect?
9. How can you show men your gratitude for the evidence you see of their good hearts?
10. What prayers would God be likely to want you to pray regarding the important man or men in your life?

CHAPTER NINE

OUR READINESS TO WORSHIP: CELEBRATING HIS COMING

I want to be God-blessed by my husband.
PAT LANDMAN

They were lying in bed that night, husband and wife, talking through some painful issues from her past she could no longer keep buried. All day they'd been exchanging those cues unique to each couple by which they come to anticipate sexual intimacy, but now their intentions had been derailed by this unexpected emotional intrusion. Gently he listened and spoke, tender words and kind. Gradually her tears and pain subsided, and she could rest.

"I feel so sad," she said as they nestled into sleep. "I'd looked forward to making love tonight."

"Oh," he replied, almost surprised, "but we *have* been making love."

To say this man knows how to bless his wife is a monumental understatement.

GOD'S COMING TO US

When good men come to us on God's behalf to bless us with their words and their glad knowledge of our hearts, God Himself comes to us and His image shines in His world. In men's coming to us and in our responsiveness to their love, we are receiving more than them—we are receiving God as well. And as we together give and receive love, we offer a joyful and mutual symphony of praise before the God who created us male and female to show forth the image of who He is. The dance of intimacy is God's own dance, and when we enter it with joy and abandon, we worship.

In worship we celebrate God's coming to us, though His coming may spark varied responses in us. Our worship may be accompanied by terror akin to the dread of the Israelites at Mount Sinai (Exodus 19), or conviction of sin such as Isaiah's "Woe is me" (Isaiah 6), or abandon that reflects Mary's anointing of Jesus (John 12). But worship always recognizes who has come, and in the coming of the everlasting God, we are drawn irresistibly to adoration and devotion.

Worship does not happen in a vacuum, of course. We worship God in the midst of life's circumstances, whether those circumstances are to our liking or not. Surely we rejoice in His goodness when the "boundary lines have fallen for [us] in pleasant places" (Psalm 16:6). Moses' sister Miriam, for example, led the Israelites in a celebratory worship dance after Pharaoh's army was destroyed (Exodus 15). But we also adore God when He comes to us in our sorrow to quiet us with His presence, or when He engages with us in our struggle to submit to His will or to understand His ways. David "went into the house of the LORD and worshiped" when he learned that the child born of his adulterous union with Bathsheba had died (2 Samuel 12:20). Such worship steadies us by grounding us in the eternal reality that supersedes the mundane details of our sometimes painful temporal existence.

God longs for us to worship Him, for as the Westminster Shorter Catechism says, the ultimate purpose of our existence is "to glorify God and to enjoy Him forever." Thus in every circumstance we may adore God in ways appropriate to where we are emotionally—we may laugh or weep, sing or groan, dance or prostrate ourselves—in keeping with our situation. Any time is a good time to celebrate God's infinite goodness, which is as irrefutable as it is immutable.

God delights in our willingness to rest in His presence, even (or perhaps especially) when our circumstances are not to our liking. Edith Schaeffer declared, "Trusting God to give us sufficient grace to face our difficult circumstances is a gift on our part to God. Satan accuses God of not having anyone who really loves Him except for what they can get from Him—a perfect spouse, a happy home, healthy children, success, or whatever. But a woman, for example, who has been disappointed in her marriage yet still trusts God and loves Him and asks Him for help—that woman brings God joy because of her trust."

As we relax in God's care for us, we gain a much-needed long-range view of life. Cynthia Heald said about trust, "We could live the rest of our lives in bitterness and hate, shriveled up inside, or we can turn to the living God and allow Him to come in. God is God, and if we will trust Him and see life from His point of view, we can have an eternal perspective and we can rest." She then added these challenging words: "God's ways are not our ways, and we sometimes find ourselves asking if God knows what He's doing. But we must come back to trusting His love, His sovereignty, and His grace."

CHANGED IN HIS PRESENCE

Women who believe God knows what He's doing and who abide in the presence of God's fierce love are profoundly changed. As we approach His presence with our hearts, God brings His own heart to us, and we are transformed by His coming. Moses' face shone; David was grieved but settled; Isaiah volunteered for the mission field; Mary was reduced to tears. Worship alters us in ways we are unable to understand or accomplish by our own most determined efforts.

It is a risk to worship, to invite God's advent to our hearts, because His goal for us is conformity to His Son's image. A friend once said to me, "One reason we don't know

God better is because to do so requires that we look at our own hearts and become willing to let God change those hearts. How many of us are ready for that kind of earthquake in our character?" Nevertheless, anyone who has seen God's face will never again be content with the status quo, the safe, the predictable, even though the alternative may likely be disruptive.

The earthquake in our character comes sometimes unexpectedly and unasked for. I remember, for instance, the day during my most intense marital turmoil when I realized I no longer loved Bill. I was sitting on our patio watching him lift weights when the stark reality hit, and as I shook my head to somehow rid myself of the horrible truth, I sensed God asking me, "Do you think *I* love this man?" My immediate inner response was, "I don't see how You can. I really don't even think You should."

Then, of course, convicted by my own arrogant words, I stood stunned before His compassionate heart, silenced into contrition. Was it any harder for God to love Bill than to love me? In my penitence my heart cried out to Him, "It is I who cannot love this man, not You. And if I am to love this man, it will have to come from You, not me." Then God smiled, for He had known all along my own love could never have been enough to sustain my relationship with Bill. In His kindness He brought me to repentance, for what I could not do in my own strength He delighted to do in me. Only through God's Spirit can we as redeemed women be aligned with His purposes in the world, and only in that way can we love with a love that is beyond ourselves.

Amazingly enough, it is in opening our hearts to receive God's undeserved favor that we see ever more clearly His own heart of passionate yearning for us. The Old Testament is replete with God's almost plaintive cry, "I love you and long to bless you—why are you turning away from Me? Come back. *Come back!*" These are the words of a forsaken lover, longing for the restoration of intimacy with the one he loves, no matter her blemish or sin.

When we respond to God's yearning after our hearts by inviting Him in, our experience is one of both terror and delight—terror because He is so holy and unmanageable, delight because we see the pleasure in His own heart toward us. "There is nothing more redemptive in the lives of God's children than to have their eyes meet the delight of their Father's eyes," said Jody Engel. "Sometimes we're so obsessed with our sin, so busy trying to atone for something that's already been atoned for, we miss how much the Lord delights in us, and then we fail to worship.

"One of the hardest things for us to imagine about our relationship with the Lord is that He delights in us," she concluded. "We can't work at delight; it just happens. We can't control or harness it. It just is."

And when we take the risk of trust, bringing our broken and compromised hearts before God's gaze, daring to believe He delights in us despite the worst we see there, our embracing of God's grace blossoms into an intimacy with Him we never dreamed of in our best days of striving to love perfectly on our own. We find ourselves not only transformed in our experience of who God is, but also fed by His banquet of love and ravenously hungry for more of His grace than we've ever tasted before.

And in our abandon to love and desire, we are utterly unable to keep our hearts from worship.

GOD'S COMING TO MEN
We covet a similar advent of God to the lives of our men. "A sovereign move of God's Spirit is stirring the hearts of men to boldly pursue Jesus Christ," says a brochure explaining the philosophy and goals of the Promise Keepers organization. These were only words—albeit encouraging words—until I attended the Promise Keepers conference described in the opening pages of this book and worshiped with the men there. I was deeply moved by my experience that weekend, my heart drawn to compassion for men's pain, to pride

for their bold stand, to enjoyment of their good hearts, to hope for their redeemed future.

I also wanted those men to go home and bless their wives and mothers and daughters in more meaningful ways than they ever had before. I wanted women everywhere to experience what Connie Schaedel described when she addressed the men at a Promise Keepers conference held in Anaheim, California, shortly after the death of her husband: "Bud was a wonderful Promise Keeper," Connie told those thousands of men, "and I am a promise reaper." We as women reap the rewards of men's redeemed hearts as they become clearer reflections of who God is relationally in a rapidly darkening world.

My hope, stirred to anticipation at that men's conference, was that God would be seen and worshiped with greater abandon than ever before because of His work in transforming men's relationships. When God shows Himself to men, He also shows Himself through them, especially to their wives. We in turn can learn to recognize in men's kind movement toward us the tender desire God Himself has for us. Christ, our heavenly Bridegroom eager to bless His bride, makes His appearance through the eyes and words and movement of good men who speak and act on His behalf. The fact that men don't love us perfectly as Christ does is beside the point; we as women, representing the as yet imperfect Church, don't respond perfectly either. But the question is, Are we willing to act toward men in such a way as to model the Church's love for and honor toward Christ, and her willingness to follow Him?

Men must struggle to model Christ to us; *our* job is to live out toward men the glad response to them that reflects the Church's dance of joy at the coming of the Bridegroom. When we yield as the bride of Christ to God's wooing heart, we are softened to rest in the hearts of men as a reflection of our trust in Christ. As men move toward us, we are to welcome them gladly (or perhaps struggle to understand why we feel unable to welcome them gladly), receiving with joy the gifts they bring.

COOPERATING WITH REVIVAL

As God's Spirit stirs men to change, however, we women will also be confronted with the unique challenge of living with "new" men committed to serving God and loving their families with involvement and gentle strength. It is, surprisingly enough, a mixed blessing. Some women have prayed for years that God would generate the spiritual renewal they're seeing in the lives of the men they love. But what they think will usher in unadulterated joy will bring with it other, unexpected emotions as well.

It's not just that Satan will fill our ears with his lie: *Don't believe it—men can't really change.* More than that, we struggle because we, too, are called to change even if men do not, and the Enemy of our souls will be ruthless to stir up our rage and self-pity with his insidious words: *Why should you have to change, especially if men won't?*

I remember what happened to me when Bill finally turned his heart back toward God and toward me, receiving God's gift of sobriety after years of alcohol abuse and relational turmoil in our marriage. His repentance was not at all what I expected.

Of course, I was delighted that my prayers and the prayers of many others who also loved Bill had been answered. Living with a repentant man had (and continues to have) joyous moments that richly bless my life. But I also experienced flashes of deep anger, and I couldn't understand why. My soul struggled with disruptive questions I could neither ignore nor fully answer.

"Why didn't God use *me* to change Bill? And why did He wait so long? Had He not seen how tired I was?

"Now that Bill has repented, how do I forgive all the years of his neglect and vacancy? What do I do with my anger now that he's emptied all the bullets of justified outrage

from the gun I'd always leveled at him? It was easy to be outraged, but how can I be sad without bitterness?

"How am I to act when he shows me his legitimate
anger? What is proper etiquette when he cries? I knew how
to manage his harshness and abandonment, but his tenderness undoes me. Why do I find it so hard to be cherished?

"Shouldn't our progress be moving faster? Why do we
still fight? And why am I angrier and more desolate than ever
when he fails me?"

I had thought Bill's repentance would be wonderful, and
it has been. But the presence of a good man in my life (that
is, a redeemed and repeatedly repentant man) continually
brings me face to face with my own entrenched commitment
to stay in control, no matter what. And God is passionately
concerned that I see how foolish and counter-productive my
control strategies are. Not only do they not keep me out of
pain; they also do not put my heart at rest, neither with God
nor with Bill. And that is what my feminine heart most
desires. I long to go off-duty with my husband and with God,
trusting God's unfailing love and Bill's softened heart of
repentance. Sadly, my anger and control sabotage the rest I
was designed to enjoy.

That is how it is with us. We say we want men's passion
for God and for us, but receiving either one puts us in a position we fear and sometimes despise: We are no longer in
charge of directing our relationships because we are called
to trust God and respond to the hearts of His repentant but
still fallen men. Bill's spiritual renewal was not an end but a
beginning—for both of us. As Bill grows in grace (in his willingness to acknowledge his sin and ask for forgiveness), the
call God issues to me is the same (that I acknowledge *my* sin
in my interactions with Bill and ask for his forgiveness). Thus
Bill's repentance, while offering me greater rest than I've
ever known, also serves the higher purpose of ushering me
into recognition of and repentance for my sin, and then into
God's grace and His rest.

The struggle wasn't over when God captured Bill's heart.

We are wrong to think spiritual revival will solve all our problems. It is more likely instead to plunge us more honestly into whatever unacknowledged problems have been there all along—not to discourage us, but to invite us into authenticity and utter dependence on God. This is holy conflict for the sake of the gospel.

Something shifts when God's Spirit enters the equation of our relational turmoil. Now that Bill is increasingly allowing God to take over his life, we fight less often *against* each other and more often alongside and on behalf of one another and our marriage, paying the price of relational disorder and learning to bring the gospel to one another in refreshingly new and wonderful ways. And our unabashed love for each other, sustained by God's grace to and through us, is more than worth the blood we shed in the keeping of our expensive vows.

CROSS YOUR HEART

One of the most important gifts men bring to us is their gift of promise keeping. Trusting in God's promises is fundamental to our faith, but being able to trust the promises of men is essential to us as well. We do not trust, of course, that men will never let us down, but that redeemed men will continue to repent when they do let us down. The primary reason I can trust Bill's movement in my life is that I know this man listens to God, and I have seen the pattern of his repentant sorrow when I show him the "blood" his sin has drawn.

Promise keeping (living with integrity) is as costly as it is important to our relationships. Little children demand, "Cross your heart and hope to die if you tell a lie," and their friends draw crosses over their hearts and utter the hope. There is a cross at the heart of every kept promise, because something has to die when promises are kept. Every man who honors his wedding vows, who cherishes his wife, who goes faithfully to work each week, who spends time with his children, who pays his bills, who deals fairly with his employees or subordinates, who does an honest day's work, who honors his contracts in business, who keeps his word to his friends, who tithes at church and is faithful in worship — those men reflect the sacrificial love Christ modeled in the shedding of His blood for His Church.

Scripture teaches there are no bloodless covenants. Jesus, the ultimate Promise Keeper, accomplished by His shed blood God's promise to redeem His people from their sin. Every kept promise requires a death — to self, to comfort, to instant gratification, to the entitlement mentality. We all shed blood in the keeping of our covenants, and we are to receive gratefully the blood men shed on our behalf.

Jane Berry gave words to her appreciation for her husband's dependable promise keeping. "Richard is a promise keeper," Jane said, "and I'll tell you what, it's important to me. He is so consistent, so drive-you-to-distraction consistent. He changeth not. Sometimes I want him to be a little more flexible and let some things go," Jane admitted, "but it's good to know I've got a man who's going to keep his word."

Our ultimate model for promise keeping, of course, is the God of the Bible. As one woman said, "There is no human being who can keep a promise perfectly. Only the Lord." It is our surest hope.

MEN BLESSING OUR LIVES

Promise keeping, however, is not the only gift men bring to us. Time and again as I have talked with women about receiving God's love through good men, I've asked them to tell me a story of how a man has blessed their lives. Good men *do* bring us their hearts of love more often than we may acknowledge or recognize. They might, for instance, say words we long to hear. Holly Phillips confided, "One of the best gifts Randy ever gave me was when he sat me down several years ago on our anniversary and asked me to forgive him for all the mistakes he had made. That did more for me in one evening than all the fifteen years previously had done."

Men's words of repentance and their words of admiration add rich blessing to our lives as women. Edith Schaeffer told me what her husband had said that blessed her life. "Fran always said, 'I don't know why it is, but when I'm speaking and you walk into the auditorium, the whole place comes alive. There isn't anything like your face. I look around the place and there isn't anyone as beautiful as you.'" Kind words from a noble man.

We honor and bless men when we receive their kindness with pleasure and gratitude. Rachael Crabb said, "Larry enjoys treating me like a queen—nothing makes the man happier. He loves to see me pleased." How true that is of good men, who reflect the Father's delight in His daughters through their own masculine eyes. And how important that we receive their delight, affirming their power to bless our lives.

Sometimes men bless us in ways that have nothing to do with romantic words. Susan Yates recognized her husband's love gift in what she called "reading my heart" when their twelve-year-old Golden Retriever had to be put to sleep because of cancer. "I'm a real 'dog person,'" Susan said, "and Johnny knew I couldn't emotionally make the decision. He read my heart and said, 'Leave it up to me.' He was wonderful, taking her to the vet, staying with her while she was put to sleep, then coming back home to make sure I was okay. I needed him to step in, and his tenderness and understanding really ministered to me."

Occasionally what we need is our husbands' intervention on our behalf as we deal with our children. Mary Farrar said that when her husband, Steve, returns from his frequent travels, he sometimes has to discipline their boys regarding their disrespect toward her. "One time," Mary said, "Steve told them, 'What your mother says *goes*. I stand behind her 100 percent, and if you don't obey her, you will know from me!' If he had bought me a hundred roses," she declared, "he wouldn't have blessed me more."

Because we are each unique, we are wrong to expect that the blessings men bring to us will look like the blessings other men bring to the women in their lives. "Dwell with [your wives] according to knowledge," the Apostle Peter instructs husbands (1 Peter 3:7, KJV). And so we must be glad to receive the blessings men *do* bring, not what we think they *should* bring. My husband, Bill, has a Ph.D. in Nancy—an intimate, studied knowledge of my soul that enables him to richly bless my life with exactly the right word or touch at just the right time. He has become expert at reading my eyes and my expressions, my sentences and my silences, my moods and my memories. This man dwells with me most wonderfully according to his intimate knowledge of me, and I would be wrong to compare his love gifts to what some other man has brought to his wife.

Along that same line, consider the words of Luci Shaw, whose first husband, Harold, died of cancer. "It's part of love to plan and to work together for the time when you and your mate may be separated by death," Luci explained. "One of the wonderful things Harold did for me before he died was to show me how to test the oil in the car and how to put storm windows up—practical things like that. He also left me a little black book in which I could find information about the cars, about the furnace, about repairmen, about legal matters, and especially about financial matters, which totally paralyze me. But Harold said, 'All right, this is hard for you, but find a person you can trust and give your checkbook to that person every month and pay to have it balanced so you'll know what your financial status is.' Those were acts of love that said to me, 'I know life is full of tragedy and I want you to have something to go on after I'm gone.'"

GOD'S COMING THROUGH GOOD MEN

There are times when our husbands show us God's face not by doing or saying anything special, but just by being who they are and doing the ordinary things that go with being responsible men. Cinny Hicks said about her husband, "I was watching Bob mow the lawn today, and I just felt this compassion come over me, realizing the burdens he bears and thinking about how so many people are counting on him. Women sometimes kill something in men by expecting them to be something they're not instead of appreciating who they are and what they have done for us." Though her husband may not even have seen it, Cinny was adoring him with her eyes.

Sometimes our husbands reveal what God is like by showing their good hearts toward our children. Jan Frank described a scenario that she received as a blessing from both her husband, Don, and from the Lord. "One night I was sitting in our den reading," she said, "when I looked up and observed my two little girls and their daddy in the living room in front of the television. Heather had taken two pillows from her room and placed one under her dad's head and the other beside him where she lay down. Kellie, the two-year-old, picked up her favorite blanket and placed it on her dad's chest where she proceeded to rest her head. Don glanced my way with a tender smile on his face as if to say, 'These are *my* girls.' To see the delight in Don's heart and the love of a good daddy was just a blessed gift. Women must not make their husband the father they never had, but in that scene I felt God showing me what His own Father-love for me was like."

Of course, women with husbands and children are not the only women who need and can receive blessings from God through good men. Sometimes those gifts come from good fathers or from someone at church. Mary Kassian tells this story of being blessed when she was a young single woman. "When I was about seventeen years old," she said, "I had a heart and passion for God and was involved in an evangelistic rock band. We would go to prisons and beaches, and we were going to convert the world.

"Rock music was taboo in our church at that time," she explained, "and a lot of people in the church criticized me for having the band. But there were two men who really affirmed me. One was my father, who hates rock music but said to me, 'As long as you love God and are seeking to serve Him, we're behind you one hundred percent.' The other was a godly older man, probably nearing his eightieth birthday, who out of the blue came up to me after church one day and put his arm around my shoulders and said, 'Mary, do you know what my philosophy is?' I said, 'No, Mr. Purdy, what is it?' And he said, 'The more drums, the better.' And he winked his eye and walked away."

Perhaps a woman's blessing will come from her son, as illustrated by this story Edith Schaeffer told about what happened to her after the death of her husband, Fran. "The first Christmas after Fran died I spent with my son Frankie and his wife," Edith said. "Frankie had told me not to do my shopping before I got there because he wanted us to shop together. He took me to a lovely place in Boston where they had cheese and wonderful bread, and then we went shopping. We had a wonderful day together—it was the greatest gift." Frankie's kindness to his mother was evidence of God's provision for Edith at a painful season in her life.

When God brings single women gifts of affirmation or kindness from men who are not their husbands, their challenge will be to receive those gifts with gratitude, not demanding more. Those gifts may not be the intimate blessings they most long for, but women who are alone can receive God's own advent through whatever He provides at the hands of any good man.

All of us, single or married, are to be on the lookout for God's coming to us through the words and kindnesses of men. And when He comes, we are to worship Him for the evidence He shows us of His good heart toward us through the compassionate words and deeds of His redeemed sons.

The heart of a woman who is learning to put her hope in God and in whatever He provides or withholds in her life—such a heart brings gladness to the heart of God. As this woman respects and desires, forgives and waits for the hearts of men, she is learning to rest in God. Such a woman is never far from worship at any given moment, ready always to see and celebrate God's work in His people's hearts. When her husband or child or friend repents, she joins the heavenly party and inwardly flings a handful of confetti. When she watches her husband mow the lawn or play with his children, she weeps for joy and tenderness, because she sees the breathtaking miracle and loveliness of common, everyday life. And when she experiences tears and brokenness in the man for whom she has prayed on her face before God, she does not fix or comfort or teach; she simply removes the sandals from her feet and worships, because she knows God is there and she stands on holy ground.

THE COMING OF THE BRIDEGROOM
Worship is the compellingly appropriate response of our hearts when we stand in the presence of God. And the more we stand in His presence, the more we long for His coming. "If not in the clouds, at least to my heart!" we cry out in our yearning. How can we bear to wait for the wedding feast of the Lamb when we shall behold Him face to face and become like Him? The Spirit groans with us and with all of creation as we await the consummation of this age, Christ's return, the Bridegroom coming to His bride, which will usher us all into the eternal NOW, where God dwells.

It is an anguish to live in the now and the not yet, waiting and hoping for what is not fully ours until Christ comes in His glory. Not only do we pine for His advent, but we long to know the story of how our life's experiences fit into God's larger picture. Kathy Peel gave this apt description of our finite understanding: "God sees the whole parade," she said, "but we can see only one float at a time."

We are caught in the confines of our finiteness. Past, present, and future are part of our existence in a way they are not a part of God's experience, except during Christ's incarnation when He was self-limited to space and time (Philippians 2). We mortals are products of our past and unable to control our future, yet hesitant to rest in the reality of our present. On the one hand we sometimes want to go back in time, to somehow redo our past so it will have a happier outcome. On the other hand, we worry about what will come in the future and spend enormous amounts of energy trying to shape it to our liking, raging all the while that we cannot control so much as the number of hairs on our heads.

But God calls us to live in the present, trusting in His care for us, one day at a time. He will not be pushed. When the time is right, when He is ready, He will come. In the meantime, we women must be patient, modeling God's "nowness" as we live not only *in* the present moment, but present to the present moment. We must learn to wait and invite, sorrow and rejoice, and relish our tastes of Home even as we groan for Christ's appearing.

And we must pray for God to come to us all. There is probably no greater gift we as women can offer God than our trust in Him to work in our lives and in the lives of the men we love. When God moves, it is always in response to the prayers He has incited His people to pray.

And because He loves us and longs passionately to come to us, God in His own time will do what He has urged us to ask of Him through His Spirit in us. Holly Phillips said, "The reason I have hope that revival will come to our nation is because for thirty and forty and fifty years women have been in their prayer closets praying. God has heard the prayers we've sent up as incense before Him. He's seen the tears we have wept over men and the pain they've caused us and our love and affection for them—He's seen it all and He's decided to move, especially among His sons. I don't know why He's chosen to do it now, but I do know His timing is absolutely perfect.

"What concerns me," Holly went on to say, "is what we women are going to do with this. My prayer is that God will awaken our hearts—our broken hearts, our angry hearts, our cold, hard hearts—that He will give us insight into what men have been up against and what we women have been up against, so our hearts can be softened and we can cooperate with Him rather than sabotage what He's doing."

It is the call to both life and death for us, for it will reveal our deepest beliefs about God—whether or not we think Him both powerful enough (Is He sovereign?) and loving enough (Is He good?) to sustain our souls no matter what our past or our future. Thus is the question of faith central to every breath we take every day of our lives. It is, in fact, the only question worth asking, and our response the only answer that ultimately matters.

And herein lies both our opportunity and our hope. We as women cannot cooperate with what God is doing and will do in and through our men until we are willing to wait in His presence and worship until He comes, allowing Him to lead us into the wilderness of our sorrow and desire so we can hear Him speak tenderly to us there (Hosea 2:14). We cannot do men's work for them, nor should we relinquish our own feminine responsiveness. Men must move and we women must receive. Both are part of the dance that reflects God's love for His bride—he to pursue (as did Jesus) and she to respond (as does the Church). Together, our dance heralds forth the love of God shed abroad, which is His glory, which is our joy.

Heart to heart connection—that is what men and women are designed to offer and receive. Created male and female to reflect the unspeakable mystery of what God Himself is like, we as God's image-bearers are invited to receive His grace so His Spirit can captivate our hearts and produce in our relationships the oneness He Himself enjoys within His own society of unity. We will desperately need God's presence with us if we are to offer our true hearts to one another. Will we stand ready to worship at the advent of our Lover whenever and however He shows us His face? If we will, a watching world will know there is a God who loves.

May the glory of the One in whose image we are
created shine forth from us like a beacon, so that our
dark and lonely world will be drawn to the embracing
warmth of the Father's gracious love. And may
Christ's Kingdom come, now and soon!

QUESTIONS FOR REFLECTION AND DISCUSSION
Recognizing that worship is central to who we are meant to
be and how we are meant to live, ponder the following
questions.

1. How varied are your emotional responses when you
   worship God?
2. What difference is there, if any, between God's coming
   to you during corporate worship (in a church service,
   for example) and during your individual worship time?
3. In what ways has your heart been changed by having
   been in God's presence?
4. How might men model Christ in coming to you?
5. What experiences have you had of worshiping God
   when a man has shown you God's face and heart?
6. What stories of women blessed by men have been
   meaningful to you? Explain.
7. What might be (or has been) the most difficult aspect
   of living with a repentant man?
8. If you find it hard to be cherished by God or men,
   explain why.
9. What changes, if any, in your relationships with men
   have resulted from your reading this book?
10. What changes, if any, in your relationship with God
    have resulted from your reading this book?

NOTES

Chapter One—Our Unquenchable Desire: Affirming God's Design
1. Joyce Clayton Morse, sidebar in an article by Anne L. Meskey in *Discipleship Journal*, Issue 79, January/February 1994, p. 34.

Chapter Two—Our Survival Devices: Distorting God's Design
1. Lance Morrow, "Men: Are They Really That Bad?" *Time*, 14 February 1994, p. 54.

Chapter Five—Our Openness Toward God: Entering Grief
1. Dr. Dan B. Allender and Dr. Tremper Longman III, *The Cry of the Soul* (Colorado Springs, Colo.: NavPress, 1994), p. 15.

Chapter Six—Our Hope in God: Relinquishing Control
1. Dale Cooper, "Proud to Bear My Father's Name," *The Banner*, 16 June 1986, pp. 8-10.

AUTHOR

Nancy Groom taught junior high English and Bible for several years after her graduation from Calvin College in Grand Rapids, Michigan. She married in 1970 and became a full-time mother in 1971. Her writing career began in 1983 as writer/editor of Sunday school, catechism, and Christian day school curriculum materials. Her first book, *Married Without Masks*, was published in 1989, followed by *From Bondage to Bonding* in 1991.

Nancy's leadership in Bible studies, support groups, conferences, and workshops over the years has put her in contact with hundreds of Christian women eager to talk with her about their joys and struggles. In preparation for writing this book she also interviewed over twenty-five women active in Christian ministry throughout North America, who shared with her the ways they have been both disappointed and blessed by men. Nancy's personal journey in learning to face with integrity the alcoholism and control strategies in her own family provides both the context and firsthand experience from which she writes about women's relationships with men.

Nancy lives with her husband, Bill, in Miami, Florida.